On any given day, we are acutely aware of life's challenges. Lindsay tackles the trials we face by pointing us to God's soul-tending grace. Her writing style flows as she provides her genuine personal perspective along with biblical stories and truths, always bringing the focus back to God's provision, care, love, and grace. Lindsay follows that with reflection/discussion questions—and response opportunities—that allow the reader to apply God's truth in daily life and give Him thanks. I am looking forward to journaling my way through this study, finding security and refreshment in God's promises, and praising Him.

-Eden Keefe, Visual Faith® Ministry coach and creative design team member

Lindsay Hausch masterfully explains the Israelites' struggle to grasp their new wilderness reality and helps the reader apply it to today's world. Our modern situation often feels like a wilderness of new and unwelcome changes. It's easy to read Exodus quickly and feel a bit superior to the complaining Israelites. Yet we, too, find ways to ignore God's amazing presence in our lives. Lindsay's insightful, interactive study gives us a closer look at what the Israelites were experiencing and how their broken, human reactions shine the message of God's grace into our own lives.

-Ursula Sohns, pastor's wife and retired English professor

God's Provision in A Wilderness World is such a comfort for those of us going through a wilderness season. Lindsay reminds us, so gently and with such encouragement, that while there will be seasons of our life filled with doubts, unknowns, trials, and loss, God's promise to never forsake us still rings true. God is here, walking alongside us. This study digs deep into the Israelites' journey and helps us see how just as God provided what they needed during their time in the wilderness, He will, and does, do that for us too.

-Faith Doerr, first grade teacher at Concordia Academy in Omaha, Nebraska, and writer of Imperfectly Perfect Living blog

Whether you find yourself in a wilderness season now, emerging from one, or eager to support a loved one navigating a time of wandering in their own personal wilderness, this study is like manna for the reader's spirit. By thoughtfully asking meaningful questions and guiding the reader directly to Scripture, Lindsay invites us to a deeper understanding of our heavenly Father as the daily bread that we truly need most. Her relatable style of speaking as practitioner (rather than expert) made me feel like I was engaging this study with a friend on the journey.

-Jennifer Hein, Leadership Essentials coaching & content leader, PLI

GOD'S PROVISION
in a
WILDERNESS WORLD

LINDSAY HAUSCH

CONCORDIA PUBLISHING HOUSE · SAINT LOUIS

For my mom and dad,
Ron and Nancy Sharp,
who taught me about Jesus
and have journeyed
with me through
many wildernesses.

Published by Concordia Publishing House
3558 S. Jefferson Ave., St. Louis, MO 63118-3968
1-800-325-3040 • cph.org

Manufactured in the United States of America

1 2 3 4 5 6 7 8 9 10   32 31 30 29 28 27 26 25 24 23

CONTENTS

Introduction

The steadfast love of the LORD never ceases;
His mercies never come to an end;
they are new every morning.

Lamentations 3:22–23

I'm not a morning person, though I wish I were. I want to be the mom who smiles and engages with my little morning birds. But first thing in the morning, my kids seldom get more than a jovial grunt from me. I need a jump start of coffee and a few quiet minutes so I can deliberately shift to a positive mood.

I think our Christian walk sometimes needs a deliberate shift too—toward gratitude. This makes me think of a line from an old favorite hymn, "Come, Thou Fount of Every Blessing," which says, "Tune my heart to sing Thy grace" (*LSB* 686:1). Often, our hearts need a little tuning to help us recognize how God is blessing us every day, just as He blessed the Israelites with manna in the wilderness.

These blessings come in ordinary ways. They also come wrapped in unexpected struggle or sacrifice. When we "give thanks in all circumstances," we begin to see our circumstances differently, as God tunes our hearts to recognize He is with us even when life is hard (1 Thessalonians 5:18).

Whether you are wandering in a wilderness season like the Israelites or going through the motions of ordinary life, be assured that God is present and providing. Gratitude helps us see where God is at work in our lives. It gives us a lens through which we recognize God's blessings, like manna, that we can touch, see, and experience. Gratitude also cultivates faith in the unattainable things our hearts hope for.

> Now faith is the assurance of things hoped for, the conviction of things not seen. For by it the people of old received their commendation. (Hebrews 11:1–2)

I pray that this study helps you wake up to God's provision and presence in your life today. Every day, no matter where we wander, God invites us to take time in His Word as we recenter our hearts on His promises and presence in our lives. Whether you are in a place of plenty or where your needs feel unmet, I pray that God meets you in this study with fresh insights and a deeper understanding of His love and provision in your life. I'm so glad we are spending this intentional time together.

How to Use This Study

You can do this study on your own or with a small group. It is broken up into eight weeks, with five Bible studies per week for a total of forty studies, but feel free to read it at your own pace.

You will see the following terms throughout the study, inviting you to pause and engage.

Write It on Your Heart

This is an opportunity to write out Scripture verses that relate to the day's reading, helping you remember them as God writes them on your heart.

Invitation

This section will help you consider how God is calling you to respond as you digest the day's content individually or discuss it as a group.

Daily Bread

This section allows you to dive deeper into God's Word for reflection.

Say Grace

This section invites you to write something you are thankful for. This phrase, from the Ecclesiastical Latin phrase *gratiarum actio*, means "thanksgiving" or "act of thanks." This can be giving thanks for something big like a healthy newborn baby or something small like your favorite flower blooming.

Lastly, this is a book for you to write in! Highlight, take notes, and leave your mark all over it! Make it personal because God's provision for you is personal. I pray that you read it and remember that God is your Healer, Provider, Guide, Savior, and Friend who longs to give you daily bread and a satisfied heart.

Let's Prepare Our Hearts Together

"And the peace of God, which surpasses all understanding, will guard your hearts and your minds in Christ Jesus" (Philippians 4:7). Someone had slipped me this verse, scrawled on a neon sticky note, during Bible study. It was an encouraging reminder that I tucked within my Bible for safekeeping.

I loved the promise of peace, but it felt fleeting, like a beautiful sunset—real and breathtaking for a moment, but in a heartbeat, melted into dusk. Nonetheless, the next time I found the note in my Bible, I took it out and taped it to my computer screen. It was a two-inch square banner of peace that I hoped would help ease the pressure of a life that felt as full as an over-inflated balloon.

There are times when we all feel that kind of pressure. We feel it with deadlines, unexpected bills, endless to-dos, and a body that aches from the force of it all. The tension of a full life can make it hard to see and appreciate all the ways God is present and providing for us each day. We cling to the hope that once we get past this deadline, over this hump, and through this season, then, yes, *then* we can experience God's peace. What begins as one hurdle can become a never-ending marathon of pressure and expectations that distract us from God's presence in our everyday lives. Even when our lives are full of good things, we sometimes struggle to slow down and calm down enough to see them. We put His promise of peace on a sticky note with good intentions to look at it later, but our distracted minds and cluttered hearts don't have the capacity to do one more thing.

God's peace becomes a finish line we reach by our own achievement rather than a promise and refuge in a moment of need. Our days are full of obligations to prepare, serve, and do all the good and worthy things we can to keep things running, but our souls begin to feel like they're running on empty. In the overwhelming and noisy world around us, we make God something for us only once we've (fill in the blank). Once we've paid the bills, met the deadline at work, cleaned the house, lost the weight, hosted

PREPARE TO RECEIVE

I think it's helpful to recognize the clutter of expectations collecting in our lives. Emotional and mental clutter sneaks in little by little until it crowds our hearts and distracts us from what matters—a life with God at the center. I want you to think of releasing the weight of worry as you rest in what God has for you in this moment. Here are some ways you can quiet your mind and prepare your heart for what God has for you today:

- Imagine you are opening a backpack and unloading the rocks that are weighing you down. As you take out each rock, name what it is and imagine placing it in the capable hands of your Father.

- Free your mind of the clutter by making a list of all the things that are distracting you right now. When you are done, pray over the list and ask God to give you freedom from it so you can be present.

- Set a timer and sit quietly in God's presence or sit still and listen to your favorite worship song (without trying to multitask and do something else).

As we release the pressure, to-dos, and anxiety filling our minds, we make room for how God wants to fill us today. I invite you to revisit this activity whenever you need a moment to ready your heart to receive what God has for you.

_____

_____

_____

_____

_____

Spend a quiet moment asking God to refresh your heart with the following Bible verses:

Create in me a clean heart, O God, and renew a right spirit within me. . . . Restore to me the joy of Your salvation, and uphold me with a willing spirit. (Psalm 51:10, 12)

I hope this prepares your heart to be filled with the good things God has for you today!

the event, or completed the project. After we've said all our prayers, gone to church, volunteered, and donated money, then we can finally experience the peace of God. The lists keep growing as we push time with God into the distance. His gift of peace and provision sits unopened because we are too stressed and distracted.

The Burden of Expectations

Our lives can get caught in the cycle of unmet expectations and an ineffable longing for something more that we can never quite achieve on our own. We try to fill the hole with all the world has to offer, but our hearts remain hungry.

I was caught in this toxic struggle even though I knew deep down that the peace of God I was yearning for wasn't available in the things of this world or my abilities. Consumerism, self-helpism, a full calendar, and a healthy dose of busyness became like the fast food I craved for a quick hunger fix. I knew that what I really needed was spiritual food for my desperate need. But in a world bursting with stuff, it felt hard to process what that food looked like.

Let's take another look at that verse on the sticky note I mentioned a moment ago. You see, as I was writing this, I took time to look up the verse in context! Here is what I discovered:

> The Lord is at hand; do not be anxious about anything, but in everything by prayer and supplication with thanksgiving let your requests be made known to God. And the peace of God, which surpasses all understanding, will guard your hearts and your minds in Christ Jesus. (Philippians 4:5–7)

Verse 7 had comforted me, but I had been looking at only half of the passage! Reading more of Philippians 4 gave me a better grasp of the message. While the admonition to "not be anxious about anything" is hard to receive on its own, the first five words of this Bible passage are the lens that transforms our view of everything: "The Lord is at hand." This doesn't deny that we have daily needs. It shows us that our needs are small matters in light of who Jesus is and what He has done. Jesus is at hand. He is not far away; He is not off doing something else more important. Jesus is not distracted by the things that are distracting us. He is at hand!

In today's western world, we face a wilderness where our spiritual needs become obscured by material consumption. There's a product, procedure, or program for every problem, want, or need, but our effort to satisfy our needs with things of this world leaves our hearts empty and aching for more.

You feel it, don't you? I imagine that's why you, dear reader, have picked up this book.

I am on a journey to cultivate gratitude and see God's everyday blessings right along with you. My soul craves Jesus. I pray for daily bread, but my human heart grumbles, doubts, and questions God's plan and provision more often than I'd like to admit. Some days, you'd be just as likely to find me browsing Amazon for things I don't need as you would to find me reading my Bible.

I believe that we are invited to recenter our hearts on the promises of Jesus—on Jesus' presence in our midst—and on God's Word, which penetrates bone and marrow *every day*. Daily, we remember our Baptism, when we were buried with Christ and raised to new life in Him. As we secure our identity to this unmovable foundation, we look to the Holy Spirit's work in our hearts, trusting that God will provide in His way, in His time, and through His means what we truly need.

Bittersweet Blessing

In this book, we will look closely at the experience the Israelites had in the wilderness. God rained down from heaven bread that was sweet like honey on starving people. For those people and us, God's manna is a gift wrapped in struggle—a bittersweet blessing of God's alien goodness kissing His people's wounds. The example of God providing manna invites us to look at our present life—with its bittersweet beauty—and see how our Creator is blessing us with His gifts in our everyday struggles. When life feels hard, we shift our thinking toward gratitude (instead of grumbling) as we acknowledge the obvious ways God is providing for us and our dear ones. Each time we pause and give thanks, we tune our hearts to recognize the blessings in all aspects and every moment of our lives.

What does manna look like in your life? It may be as simple as the jump start of coffee in your mug or the cat on your lap and as complicated as the friends who bring you homemade meals as you battle cancer or a breakthrough conversation with your teenager with whom you have a tenuous relationship. Looking for God's everyday blessings, we ground ourselves in our present provision rather than our future worries, positioning our hearts to see what God is doing in our midst. Manna reminds us that God's mercies are new every morning. Just as dew refreshes the landscape, God refreshes and feeds our souls.

God's Gifts Are Always Available

Sin entered God's creation, touching our lives with chaos and brokenness that intrudes in the form of everyday struggles. But we don't have to stay in our disillusioned stupor, staring at the pieces of our broken circumstances. God invites us to elevate our gaze to Jesus. On this side of the story, we know that God sent His Son, Jesus, to live a perfect life in our place, suffer and die on our behalf as the perfect guilt offering, and rise victorious three days later.

No matter our life circumstances, on this side of the story, we have the promise of eternal life, the promise of forgiveness and God's indwelling Spirit through Baptism, and the very presence of God in His Word and the Holy Supper Jesus instituted.

As we ask God for eyes to see our everyday blessings, we remember His unchanging gifts, which are made available to us through Jesus.

Seeing His Gifts Today

I want to be the chipper girl who always sees the glass as half full. But I'm actually the girl who has to wrestle and pin her own worry and resentment to make room for gratitude and a softer heart. You might have the same struggles. As we walk through this study, I encourage you to be honest with yourself and vulnerable with others. We aren't trying to be perfect in this process. We can't be. Instead, we admit our imperfections, lean into God's Word, and lean on one another as we soften into gratitude and recognize His provision in our lives today.

Before we begin, I ask you to take a deep breath. This study isn't about you doing something for Jesus, so don't feel like you need to hurry through the readings to prove your piety. Rather, I invite you to take your time soaking up His Word, which falls fresh on your heart today like manna, as the Holy Spirit gives you eyes to see the ways God is providing for you at this moment.

I am giving thanks for you, dear reader.

—Lindsay

WEEK 1

What Is It? Eyes
to See God's Provision

At twilight you shall eat meat, and in
the morning you shall be filled with bread.

Then you shall know that I am the LORD your God.

Exodus 16:11–12

———

An Unfamiliar Gift

Imagine receiving a gift from someone you love. A smile tugs at his mouth as your fingers tug at the ribbon to unknot the bow. His eyebrows raise in expectation as you tear the gilded paper to uncover—what, exactly? You know it's supposed to be a present that makes you gasp with appreciation, but it feels disappointing. The gift isn't what you expected—and worse, it's unrecognizable. After an awkward silence, you ask, "Umm . . . thanks! But what is it?" And secretly, you think, *I'm not sure I want this.*

It's hard to feel grateful for a gift you don't recognize. A gift from someone you love is not just a trinket wrapped in paper but a way he shows that he "gets" you. Typing this, I think of a friend who gives me pumpkin candles for my January birthday because she knows it's a scent I love year-round. There is something special about opening a gift you've been anticipating without ever having to tell the person you wanted it. You feel known and loved.

Since God is all knowing, He can predict what we will want and need. However, sometimes we hope and pray for something only to feel dissatisfied with what God gives us. His answers to my prayers are often wrapped in struggle, uncertainty, waiting, and learning to rely on Him more. The Bible tells us that God gives good gifts:

> If you then, who are evil, know how to give good gifts to your children, how much more will your Father who is in heaven give good things to those who ask Him! (Matthew 7:11)

But the knowledge of God's goodness and provision doesn't always sink into our hearts when we are enduring setbacks and disappointment. This narrative of humans trying to recognize God's goodness in the face of their doubt, confusion, or fear is seen throughout the Bible.

Can you relate to this tension? The Christian life can be a tug-of-war between recognizing our abundant God while also feeling the yank of our human hearts that ache with unmet needs, disillusionment, and longing for more. As we live in the push and pull of a life filled with God's goodness and the brokenness of sin, it is tempting to scratch our heads and think, *Lord, I'm not sure I want this.* Sure, we know there are seasons when God's blessings are bountiful, but we aren't certain how to deal with those stretches that leave us winded and wondering if God is as present in our suffering as He is when life is going our way.

I'd like to think that I'm the girl that keeps the faith even in the face of disappointment, but a little self-reflection leads me to question if I would be one of the faithful and obedient characters in the Bible or the one to grumble and question God's good gifts as fatigue and doubt poked holes in my resolve.

If you've read the Book of Exodus, you are familiar with the Israelites, who grumble when things don't go their way. Like He did with the Israelites, God often shifts my perspective as He answers my prayers in ways I don't expect—in ways that stretch me to rely more on Him. When the Israelites feel God has abandoned them and left them to starve, He rains down manna. As God blesses them with food in heaven's mysterious wrapping, He teaches them a rhythm of reliance on Him. The story of God providing manna also invites us to lean in, look closer, and see the miracle of God's provision in our midst in ways we don't expect.

The Gift of Manna

It has been only a month and a half since the Israelites' miraculous deliverance from Egypt and Pharaoh. Yes, a month and a half into their journey to the Promised Land, the Israelites wonder how wilderness wandering is better than being enslaved in Egypt. They are hungry and angry.

The term we use these days is *hangry*. My version of hungry is having a late lunch, so I truly can't relate, and I can't help but feel a little exasperated with these guys. After recently seeing all that God was capable of, you'd think they'd have a little trust. If I'm honest, though, on a grumpy day, grumbling is my specialty too. I can be pretty quick to freak out when things aren't going my way, even though God has proven faithful to me time and time again.

The good news is that God *is* patient. He doesn't get mad at their bad attitude and lack of trust. Instead, God tells Moses He will send down a gift. Not just a one-time gift but a daily provision of bread from heaven:

Then the LORD said to Moses, "Behold, I am about to rain bread from heaven for you, and the people shall go out and gather a day's portion every day." (Exodus 16:4)

God rained down sweet flakes of bread on hungry people. But rather than telling us how the people shouted "thank You!" and "alleluia," Exodus tells us they asked a question:

And when the dew had gone up, there was on the face of the wilderness a fine, flake-like thing, fine as frost on the ground. When the people of Israel saw it, they said to one another, "What is it?" For they did not know what it was. And Moses said to them, "It is the bread that the LORD has given you to eat." (Exodus 16:14–15)

The miraculous bread from heaven is named after the question on the lips of the Israelites. *Manna* is Hebrew for "What is it?" Their question demonstrates that God's amazing provision can easily be misunderstood, unrecognizable, and maybe even unappreciated in the mess and stress of our earthly circumstances. Let the Israelites' experience sink into your heart today as God guides us to take time to recognize the gifts He is providing for us. This may look like

- a flat tire (ugh!) and a generous servant who helps you get back on your way;

- a difficult diagnosis and prognosis that also offers a powerful testimony of God's goodness and provision in the midst of the struggle; or

- job loss that results in new employment that pays less but is more satisfying.

Can you think of other examples?

We, too, can fail to recognize how God is showing up in our lives and providing for our needs. Perhaps it's because we see blessing as a life free of trouble with God meeting our needs in the ways *we* expect. The Israelites have to learn to see God's goodness and glory amid their struggles. They also have to learn to see His provision in unfamiliar yet miraculous ways such as a road through a choppy sea, bread from heaven in a desolate wilderness, and bitter water transformed into sweet sustenance.

God doesn't only want to fill His people's bellies. He wants to woo their hearts for a relationship with Him. How can we relate to the Israelites' confusion when God gives us something different from what we hope for? When we ask "What is it?" how does God challenge us to stop staring at our outward circumstances and look to Him instead?

The account of God providing manna prompts us to look at the blessings God rains upon us in our landscapes of struggle and uncertainty as we learn to rely on Him for daily bread.

INVITATION

Are there ways God has provided for you that have also been a source of frustration or confusion, prompting you to ask, "What is it?" Record your thoughts here.

Was there a time God blessed you but you didn't recognize it until after the fact?

DAILY BREAD

Read Exodus 16:1–13. Notice how the Israelites fail to recognize what God is doing in their midst. Try to put yourself in their difficult circumstances and consider how you might respond. Record any observations here.

SAY GRACE

Give thanks to the LORD, for He is good,
for His steadfast love endures forever. (Psalm 136:1)

Living in the Question

I shimmied up the steep incline until I got to the round curve.

Step by step, my hands and feet gripped the tall, smooth surface until I found a flat place on top to rest my weary body.

Behind me was the treacherous climb; before me, a downward slope ended sharply.

I didn't know how I'd get beyond this spot where I rested.

From up here, I could see every breathtaking possibility. The landscape beyond was beautiful and bewildering, depending on how I looked at it. All I knew, for now, was that I needed to rest because I'd need endurance for whatever journey was ahead.

This is something I wrote and titled "Sitting atop a Question Mark." At the time, my husband, Nathan, and I were living in an open-ended question. We'd begun to feel that the place we were living and serving wasn't where we belonged long-term. Then, something happened that confirmed our feelings and propelled us to look at what possibilities God had in store for us in the future.

As we looked at options, we'd find ourselves becoming attached to different opportunities and then be disappointed when they didn't work out. We sometimes wanted to force a decision because it was easier to have answers than to live with an uncertain future. "A plan" gave us fake security and false hope to tether our hearts to. But deep down, we knew God wasn't directing us to accept any of the available opportunities. Deep down, we knew He was leading us to say no to three potential job offers even though there was no future for us in our present situation. In obedience, we declined all of them and waited on God to reveal what He had for us, anchoring our hearts to Him and trusting in His future for us.

On this side of the question, where things are resolved and God's goodness is evident, I wonder why my emotions were so raw back then. Why did my trust in God feel more like a white flag of resignation than a battle cry of hope? Revisiting this poem, however, helps me remember how scary and vulnerable it feels to wait on God for answers. I imagine you know what it feels like to sit atop a question mark, whether you are waiting for the doctor to call with results, clarity on what to do next, or the right job to come along. You understand the painful point of a question in your heart as you try to forgive a betrayal or wait for someone to forgive you. You know that an unanswered question can feel like an eternity is passing in just two minutes while you wait for the result of a pregnancy test or await a call from your teenager who has stayed out past his curfew.

We can trust in God's goodness when our circumstances are uncertain. We can't trust that the outcome will be good according to our human understanding, but we can always trust that God is good, even in hard things, and that each experience can shape us into the people He created us to be.

Pray: Father, the space of uncertainty can make us feel scared, doubtful, and unable to move forward with the confidence we crave. We pray that You would kindle our faith to hope confidently in the future we cannot yet see, trusting that You are always good and will always provide what we truly need. In Jesus' name. Amen.

Trust as a Verb

While we all have a general idea of what the word *trust* means, let's pause to unpack that word a little.

The word *trust* means "to place confidence in" or "to hope or expect confidently."

How would you define the word *trust* in your own words? Write your own definition below.

What does the Bible say about trust? Look up Proverbs 3: 5–6.

Trust in the Lord with all your heart and lean not on your own understanding. In all your ways acknowledge Him and He will make your paths straight.

Look up Psalm 9:10.

The Lord is a refuge for the oppressed, a stronghold in times of trouble.

The word *trust* can be used as a noun or a verb. What a difference the syntax makes! Often, we think of trust as a decision we make once then put on a shelf. However, I love thinking of trust as a verb that is constantly in a state of action—something we actively put into practice. While the Holy Spirit inspires, encourages, and sustains our faith walk, trust is a choice we return to when circumstances threaten to undermine the spiritual truths we put our confidence in.

The Israelites have every reason to trust that God will get them out of challenging situations. Only a chapter before, they walked through a sea that God divided. Talk about a faith-defining moment! But when they run out of food reserves and face increasingly difficult circumstances in the second month of their journey, the Israelites forget who God is and what He is capable of! Despite their lack of trust, God still provides. The only problem is that God's provision isn't what they expect or recognize. God rains down bread from heaven, and they ask, "What is it?"

God creates an opportunity for the Israelites to strengthen their trust muscles by providing in ways that are outside of their expectations. When

God instructs the Israelites to collect only the bread they need for one day, He is teaching them to trust Him one day at a time.

How is God strengthening your "trust muscles" as you rely on His provision day by day? In my season of uncertainty, I learned to view the unknown future as an exercise to trust God boldly. Rather than giving into powerless anxiety, I'd give myself ten minutes to cry and be upset. Then I'd wipe off the mascara smears and say, "Okay, God. I'm excited to see what You're up to next."

Like the Israelites, as we sit in the tension of unanswered questions, we are invited to rely on God more fully and look to Him to provide, even when we don't understand how He will or what His provision will look like. We trust in the assurance that as His ways are higher, His means are better, and the story isn't over until Jesus comes and makes all things new.

Give us faith to trust you boldly;
Hope, to stay our souls on you;
But, oh, best of all Your graces,
With Your love our love renew.

(*LSB* 851:4)

INVITATION

Can you remember a time when you had to wait on God for answers? Describe it below.

What did you learn about trust in this experience that you would like to remember?

DAILY BREAD

Read Matthew 6:25–34. How does Jesus encourage you to trust God in uncertain times?

SAY GRACE

We praise You, O God, our Redeemer, Creator;
In grateful devotion our tribute we bring. (*LSB* 785:1)

WEEK 1: DAY 3

Doubting God's Answer

Have you ever given your all to a cause you care about—your church, your job, a friend—only to feel unseen or unappreciated? Have you ever felt like you did the right thing, but ultimately, it wasn't worth it?

The Israelites do everything the Lord tells them to do as they leave Egypt. They slaughter lambs and put the lambs' blood on their door frames. They roast the lamb meat with bittering herbs and eat it with unleavened bread. They tuck their cloaks in their belts with their sandals on their feet and eat in haste. They ask the Egyptians for silver and gold and leave quickly in the middle of the night with their unleavened dough. They take the long desert road and cross the Red Sea, all according to God's instruction. They reach the other side of the Red Sea after a long and tedious journey. Their bread is long gone, and they are hungry! They may be thinking something like, "We did our part, God! Now, where's the food?"

We can run into the trap of looking at God as a vending machine. Do you know those machines that have all that delicious junk food? We find what we want—a Snickers bar or those peanut butter–filled, neon orange crackers—then slide in the money, hit the button, and *voila!* What we crave drops in front of us. God knows what we want, but He is also the wise Father who knows what we need.

It seems as though the Israelites are following God's instructions but lack trust in His character and respect for His authority.

On day two, we looked at the meaning of *trust*—"to place confidence or hope in something or someone." Today we will explore what respect looks like in our relationship with God as we acknowledge His authority.

The word *respect* means "to consider worthy of high regard."

How would you define *respect* in your own words?

What do you think it means to respect God's authority?

Resetting Our Hearts

In the simplest of terms, respecting God's authority means acknowledging

H E I S G O D; i a m n o t.

The lowercase letter *i* is intentional. I had to go back and change my settings on my computer to be able to type a lowercase letter *i*. Autocorrect insisted I capitalize it. This is also the default setting of my sinful heart, which wants to make my self, my will, and my authority bigger than God's.

Why is respecting God's authority important? As we begin to comprehend who God is, He invites us to loosen our grip on what we desire from Him and cultivate a hunger for what He desires for us. Our transactional, vending-machine relationship no longer satisfies the hunger stirred in us as we begin comprehending His sovereignty, power, provision, and sacrificial love.

The Book of Job is a great detour as we pursue a deeper understanding of God's ultimate power and authority. In the Book of Job, God reveals Himself as the "Holy who." Job asks, "Why, God, has my life been ruined?" God answers not by explaining *why* but by giving Job a glimpse of the vastness of *who* He is.

Let's unpack a little of who God is together. Look up the following verses in your Bible.

Job 38:2: Who is this that darkens _my counsel_ by words without _knowledge_ ?

Job 38:8: Who _shut up the_ _____ the sea with _____ _doors_ _____ ?

Job 38:36: Who has put _wisdom_ in the _heart_ _____ or given _understanding_ to the _mind_ ?

When we pray and wait for answers, justice, a favorable prognosis, forgiveness, or reconciliation . . .

When we are weary of waiting for the baby we've prayed for, the relief our body aches for, the breakthrough we've been looking for . . .

We, like the Israelites, may be tempted to grumble, tell God all the reasons we deserve His blessing, or, like Job, ask God why. But today, we remember who God is and train our hearts to respect His authority and sovereignty. It is in light of who God is that we are better able to answer the following questions:

Who has the best plan for our lives?

Who heals our broken bodies and relationships?

Who speaks, "Peace! Be still" (Mark 4:39) in life's storms?

Who waters the crops that grow into the food we eat?

Who loves and forgives us so that we can love and forgive others?

Who makes "everything beautiful in its time" (Ecclesiastes 3:11)?

We see cause and effect in so much of our lives that it might be hard to wrap our minds around the reality that God does not just respond to our needs but initiates the relationship. Our God is more vast and more powerful than we can comprehend, yet He humbled Himself and sacrificed His life for us. It is hard to understand God, who we don't create with our own hands or in our own image but who created us. Respecting God's authority is more than just accepting Him as our God. It is about acknowledging that we are weak, sinful, and in need of a Savior.

INVITATION

When do you need to remember the phrase "HE IS GOD; i am not"?

What comes to mind when you think about respecting God? Do other authority figures come to mind? How does that influence your understanding of the word *respect*?

DAILY BREAD

Read Romans 5:6–8. How does God reveal who He is to us in Jesus? How does this help you in wilderness seasons?

SAY GRACE

I thank You that You have answered
me and have become my salvation. (Psalm 118:21)

The Fullness of God

When I think about God's glory, I can better understand people's paralyzed response to God in the Bible. Let's just say that if God's glory, or *kābôd* in Hebrew, showed up today, an announcement for people to turn off their cell phones wouldn't be necessary. They would drop their phones and be in awe of His presence.

My husband compares God's glory appearing to Michael Jordan showing up at a rec basketball game. Everyone is surprised and excited and holds their breath to see which team he plays on and what might happen.

- *Kābôd* means "weight or significance." Think of a person who has "weight" in our society—meaning they have great influence or are worthy of respect.

- *Kābôd* also means "splendor, magnificence, or brilliance."[1]

- These words are often used to describe light.

How would you describe your understanding of God's glory?

On day three, we read about Job's question to God and God's revelation of who He is. Today, in a closer look at God's response to the Israelites grumbling for food, we see that He again gives them a wider view as He reveals His *kābôd* to them:

Then Moses said to Aaron, "Say to the whole congregation of the people of Israel, 'Come near before the LORD, for He has heard your grumbling.' " And as soon as Aaron spoke to the whole congregation of the people of Israel, they looked toward the wilderness, and behold, the glory of the LORD appeared in the cloud. (Exodus 16:9–10)

Instead of being angry with their grumbling, God reveals to them who He is and what He is capable of. God tells the Israelites to live in dependence, trust, and relationship with their Creator, even in difficult circumstances when they are anxious, afraid, and question His reliability. Again and again, God shows them that He is trustworthy and good. On Mount Sinai, Moses asks to see God's glory, perhaps as proof that God is with His people. But because Moses cannot see the fullness of God's glory and live, God lets Moses see His goodness and compassion for the people (see Exodus 33:18–19). It is easy to get lost in the anger and punishment of the Old Testament and lose sight of the fact that God is good and loves His people! He wants them to know His goodness.

Read Exodus 34:6. As God passed by, He revealed His character to Moses. What are we to know about God from this verse?

Compassionate, gracious, slow to anger abounding in love + faithfulness

With mercy and patience, God responds to the Israelites' grumbling by showing up to renew their faith. He redirects their gaze from their human need toward His splendor, authority, and power. It is similar to children staring sadly at a dried-up puddle when an ocean is in front of them. In the presence of His glory, God's people respond in humility, repentance, and fear. When God shows up, He rearranges the landscape, and our priorities are reoriented in light of His glory.

His Glory Is Everywhere

Do you get caught up in the list of things you need or ways your life is falling short? Have you ever gotten stuck in the rut of worrying and complaining about your present circumstances so much that you forget to pray or remember God's presence? For me, grumbling can become a bad habit and a mindset. I can get on a roll, singing a dirge of all the ways my life is going wrong. I love that God didn't reprimand the Israelites or even defend Himself to them. He just showed up. God's glory was the great reset button for them as they remembered their smallness and His greatness.

Just as God revealed Himself to the Israelites to encourage their faith in Him, when it feels like we are falling short, God shows up in visible and tangible ways. We can be confident that God reveals Himself to us through the power of the Holy Spirit

- in His Holy Supper, when we touch and taste the bread and wine—Jesus' body and blood shed for us;

- in the waters of Baptism, where He makes us His children; and

- in His Word, where He teaches and touches our hearts anew each time we hear it.

God's presence and glory are also written in the works of His hands. What do these verses about God's creation show us about the qualities of God?

Psalm 8:1, 3–4 *Creation of the heavens reflect God's glory*

Psalm 19:1 *We see God through His creation.*

Romans 1:20 *God's great power + glory*

Jesus instructs His disciples to look at creation, saying, "Look at the birds of the air. . . . Consider the lilies of the field, how they grow" (Matthew 6:26, 28–29). Those verses prompt us to look up, gaze all around, and see Him in the evidence of His work. We can look to the places God promises He will be: in His Sacraments, in His Word, in our hearts through the Holy Spirit, and in His creation. In these things, we remember that even when we don't see God provide for us in the ways we hope, we can still see and experience God's provision in these realities. When we, like the Israelites, are busy looking at our own life circumstances, God prompts us to look up and encounter His glory. The work of His hands is all around us.

INVITATION

How is God nudging you to look up from your present circumstances to remember His glory?

DAILY BREAD

Read John 1:4–18. How does God choose to send His glory to us? How does this transform the way we live our lives as Christians?

SAY GRACE

Be exalted, O God, above the heavens!
Let Your glory be over all the earth! (Psalm 57:11)

WEEK 1: DAY 5

Bread of Life

About 1,600 years after God sent manna to the Israelites, Jesus feeds 5,000 men, plus women and children, with five loaves of bread and two fish (see John 6:1–14). After this miraculous encounter, the crowd is eager to make Jesus their king.

If I were Jesus' publicity coordinator, I'd advise Him to go for the finale—maybe whip up another miraculous meal and wrap up with some supernatural fireworks. But rather than riding on the crowd's enthusiasm, Jesus calls them out for their impure motives, saying, "You are seeking Me, not because you saw signs, but because you ate your fill of the loaves" (John 6:26).

Jesus discerns that the people don't see Him as the Messiah but as a meal ticket. When He tells them about the "food that endures to eternal life" from the Son of Man (John 6:27), the crowd is eager for another miracle and asks, "Then what sign do You do, that we may see and believe You?" indicating that their faith hinges on what Jesus can do for them and not on who He is. "Our fathers ate the manna in the wilderness," they say, with the not-so-subtle suggestion that maybe Jesus could rain down some bread like Moses did (6:30–31). Jesus reminds them that it is God, His Father, who sends bread from heaven. Then Jesus drops a truth bomb that challenges the crowd's loyalty to Him. He says *He* is "the bread of life" (6:35) that came "down from heaven" (6:38). The bread the people eat their fill of looks way more appealing than this "bread from heaven" (6:32) Jesus is describing, and they can't wrap their minds around His words. But Jesus doesn't stop there. He says something that is downright offensive:

> Whoever feeds on My flesh and drinks My blood has eternal life, and
> I will raise him up on the last day. (John 6:54)

To Christians who grew up learning about the Sacrament of Holy Communion, the real presence of Jesus' body and blood in the bread and wine of the Holy Supper is meaningful and miraculous. But when many Jewish people hear they should eat Jesus' flesh and drink His blood for eternal life, they are disgusted. These are people who follow hundreds of Jewish laws. They refrain from eating certain foods and meat until after they drain it of its blood. Then Jesus tells them this! This man of miracles is making audacious and polarizing claims. As the stakes of following Him get higher, His disciples are confronted with a question: Are we here for His miracles or because He is the true Messiah?

God Has the Answers, Even When We Don't

We look to Exodus 16 again and remember that the Israelites had asked a question when they first encountered the manna: "What is it?" In accepting this bread from heaven, they submit to God to sustain them in a wilderness where they cannot sustain themselves. Both the Israelites and the crowd in Capernaum are amazed and confounded as they get a glimpse of God, who is mysterious and personal. This almighty God woos their hearts, yet He offends their minds. Are they hungry enough to accept the bread that ultimately satisfies them and rely less on their own understanding? One thing is for sure: they know that following God means change and transformation.

Many of us live a full and satisfying life with a side of Jesus on Sundays until we encounter a need the world cannot satisfy—the loss of a loved one, a need for healing, or a broken heart. In these wildernesses, we, like the Israelites and the crowd in Capernaum, are forced to wrestle with questions about God that spill into not just what we do but who we are. These questions should be familiar from previous days. *Even when I don't understand, do I trust Jesus' character and believe His promises? respect His authority in my life?*

With Jesus at the center of our lives, we can trust that He is willing and able to satisfy our needs. However, even when we fall short and look to other things to satisfy us, Jesus still comes to us, pursues us, and offers Himself to us. Even when our hearts feel uncertain and unsatisfied, Jesus comes. He promises that we can find Him in His Holy Supper and in God's Word. We rest assured in our Baptism that even though we are entirely flawed, sinful humans, "the Spirit of Him who raised Jesus from the dead dwells in you" (Romans 8:11). As we wake every day and feel the ache of this world and the temptation to measure our worth by our homes, bank accounts, and weight on the scale or to look to Amazon, Hobby Lobby, or a Starbucks drive-through to satisfy our needs, we can return to the truth of Jesus that satisfies and redeems our imperfect hearts and gives us ultimate purpose.

Our emotions will shift in a changing world, but we can remember the bread of life, Jesus, who satisfies us when our earthly needs are unmet. God guides the Israelites to look to Him as their provider and not just the one who dispenses miracles, in the same way that Jesus reveals He is the bread the people need. As we look to God to satisfy our needs, we see His ultimate desire for us is to delight in Him. When His mystery and glory cause us to wonder, we open our hearts to God, who is greater than our imagination. In this life, we will face uncertainty and unanswered questions, but when we trust that God loves us, we can walk boldly in His promises and blessings for our lives.

Daily Bread and Food for Thought

I created an acronym, which you will see on the next two pages, to remind us what Jesus, the bread of life, means for us and to help us consider the ways He is inviting us to respond today.

BELIEVE

Jesus said to them, "I am the bread of life; he who comes to Me will not hunger, and he who believes in Me will never thirst." (John 6:35)

What is God inviting you to believe (about Himself, about who you are) today?

REPENT

And Peter said to them, "Repent and be baptized every one of you in the name of Jesus Christ for the forgiveness of your sins, and you will receive the gift of the Holy Spirit." (Acts 2:38)

The word *repent* means "to turn around or change your mind." What is God inviting you to change your mind about today?

EAT

But He answered, "It is written, 'Man shall not live by bread alone, but by every word that comes from the mouth of God.'" (Matthew 4:4)

What truth from His Word does God want you to remember today?

ASK

Your Father knows what you need before you ask Him. Pray then like this: "Our Father in heaven, hallowed be Your name. Your kingdom come, Your will be done, on earth as it is in heaven.

Give us this day our daily bread." (Matthew 6:8–11)

How is God inviting you to pray today? Is there a need burdening your heart that you haven't asked Him to provide for?

DISCIPLE

And He said to them, "Follow Me, and I will make you fishers of men." (Matthew 4:19)

How is God inviting you to walk closer with Him as you point others to Jesus?

SAY GRACE

For from Him and through Him and to Him are all things.
To Him be glory forever. Amen. (Romans 11:36)

WEEK 2

God Is Our Guide

He rebuked the Red Sea,
and it became dry,
and He led them through
the deep as through a desert.

Psalm 106:9

———

Look Up

When you're traveling through unknown territory, you need a trust-worthy guide. I learned that during the fall of my senior year in college when I traveled to Marrakech, Morocco, with five other classmates. My parents agreed to let me go under the pretense that an adult chaperone would join us.

I didn't think we needed a chaperone, but God knew better.

On our first day in Morocco, we met Mohammed, our taxi driver. His full beard couldn't hide his baby face as he smiled wide and shared stories of his two grown sons and teenage daughter.

"I wouldn't want my daughter traveling alone in this city," he said as he pulled up to our hotel. "I would like to drive you while you're here. I'll make sure you're safe."

As independent college girls, we were cavalier about his concern, but he seemed genuine and knowledgeable about the city. Plus, he had a car, so we gladly accepted the offer. We didn't know then that Mohammed would be the mannalike gift God would provide in our time of need in the desert.

It all began when we heard from the hotel concierge that we could hire tour guides to take us on camels across the Sahara Desert for a small fee. We would go to an oasis in the middle of the desert, where we'd have a warm Moroccan meal and camp overnight. If it sounds too good to be true, that's because it was. But the girls and I pooled our money and agreed to the excursion.

The next day, when we gushed to Mohammed about our planned trip, he suggested we pay him to come along as our chaperone. He said we'd be grateful to have his vehicle to return in (apparently, riding a camel can get uncomfortable), plus, he could keep an eye on us. In the interests of our college student–size budget, we declined.

We set off with high hopes, but after a couple of hours in the desert with no civilization in sight, our tour guides began to look at us more boldly and make disrespectful gestures. The desert became pitch black at sunset, and we felt less like they were our guides and more like our captors. The promised oasis was a crudely erected tent. We huddled in the cold darkness, eating watery soup rather than the "exquisite Moroccan meal" they had promised us. We started wondering why we had agreed to let three strange men be our guides through a vast and secluded desert. We joked that it would be our last meal, but only because the truth of the situation we'd put ourselves in was too frightening to admit out loud.

Then, as we finished our meal, we heard a vehicle and saw approaching headlights. Mohammed was behind the steering wheel with a proud papa smile. He repeated that phrase about never letting his daughter go out alone, and he wouldn't let us go alone either. He exchanged words with our guides in a tongue that sounded harsh, though we couldn't understand what was said. He slept across the threshold of our tent. And in the morning, we were grateful to climb into his vehicle and let him drive us back to the safety of our hotel. God sent us Mohammed, the chaperone we needed after all.

That desert desperation helped me recognize my daily need for the Lord's guidance and discernment. Although I choose not to stumble in the dark with strangers and fall for oasis promises these days, I have learned that before I follow someone into an unknown place, I need a trustworthy guide.

The Israelites had God as their trustworthy guide. The Book of Exodus describes how God made Himself visible to them in a pillar of cloud and a pillar of fire as He led them through the wilderness: "And the LORD went before them by day in a pillar of cloud to lead the way, and by night in a pillar of fire to give them light, so as to go by day and night" (Exodus 13:21).

Because we were so focused on the adventure we craved, my college friends and I failed to recognize the way that God had chosen to provide for us by sending Mohammed. In the same way, the Israelites overlook God's goodness as He dwells among them and instead set their hearts on the oasis they want to reach. God promises them a land flowing with milk and honey, so they look to the destination as proof of God's goodness rather than seeing God Himself as the greatest blessing.

Are you walking through a desert season now? Do you feel disconnected from your community, weary from work, or longing for a destination you haven't yet reached? Are you on a challenging journey, facing some unexpected potholes, twists, or turns in your way? Or maybe you are at a crossroads and don't know which path you're supposed to take. In a world of memes, videos, and blogs, it's easy to look for guidance on social media and follow our own agendas to determine the way ahead. It's easy to pretend for a while that we're the ones in charge of our lives. That is, until the thing we didn't plan for happens and we need a lifeline to pull us out of our circumstances.

Faith gives us an airlift when the path ahead becomes impassable. In the wilderness, the Israelites learned they couldn't survive without God as their guide and provider. But in our modern world, our need for Him feels less apparent.

Today, we don't have a pillar of cloud or fire, but we have God's Word, which point us to Jesus, our lifeline, and the Holy Spirit, who works faith in us to grab onto Jesus. Jesus invites us to depend on God as we look to Him to bear the weight of our lives and guide us along the road He sets for us. Through Jesus, God's Spirit makes a home in our hearts and becomes our comforter and guide. Wherever we are in life, the account of the Israelites in the wilderness prompts us to ask ourselves if we will take Jesus' yoke and follow Him even if we don't know where He is taking us.

I don't usually know where God is taking me, but I'm learning that I need to rest in Him.

INVITATION

Can you think of five qualities that make a trustworthy guide?

1. *knowledgable*

2. *dependable*

3. *caring*

4.

5.

Which of these qualities is God inviting you to remember about His character today as you navigate life? *dependable*

DAILY BREAD

Let's look up the following verses and note what they say about God as our guide.

John 16:13
guiding

Romans 8:14
leading

Psalm 119:105 *Your word is a light to my feet and a light that guides me*

SAY GRACE

And they sang responsively, praising
and giving thanks to the LORD, "For He is good,
for His steadfast love endures
forever toward Israel." (Ezra 3:11)

A Better Guide

"If it seems too good to be true, it probably is."

We've all heard that adage. The problem is I have been slow to follow it. I have been eager to look for the ten steps, the how-to book, the program, the expert, or even the well-meaning friend to offer a quick fix or formula for a problem that, in reality, needs more than a surface fix. I crave resolution—and there's nothing like a solid plan to allay my fears.

The kids aren't listening and are acting rebellious! Not to worry. Here's a book with all the answers.

Is your cholesterol high? Take this medication.

Does your marriage feel disconnected? Sign up for this free online course.

Some resources are helpful for situations like these. Still, when it comes to spiritual matters, we can often fall into a rabbit hole of information without considering the heart transformation we need to solve the problem.

When I was a copywriter in marketing, the motto was always "Offer consumers a solution!" We are programmed to look for solutions to problems in our lives. Our culture has many guides: astrologers, nutritionists, therapists, yogis, life coaches, and influencers. All are willing to offer a compass to direct our lives (for a small fee). Suppose we don't intentionally select a guide. In that case, our desires, even our desires for good things— the promotion, the house renovation, the sales goal, the weight loss plan, the retirement—will be what direct our decisions rather than God Himself.

None of these things are bad, but when they direct our every thought or decision, they can take the place of God in our lives.

I found a throw pillow in a big retail store with the word *hope* and a definition embroidered on it: "to place trust in life's plan." That sounds like a shallow definition to me!

How would you define hope? Hope means . . .

If the plan is what we hope for, what sustains us when it fails? The only way to find soul satisfaction is to anchor our hearts to the source of abundance and satisfaction—Jesus.

Write It on Your Heart

Look up Titus 3:7. *His Grace has made us right with God, so now we have received the hope of eternal life as God's children.*

Paradise Parlayed

The Israelites are ready for God's big reveal. They'd seen Him perform miracles to deliver them from Egypt, they'd taken all of the prescribed steps, and they are finally free and ready for God to take them to freedom! But God takes them the long way. He takes them down the desert road to the Red Sea rather than the quicker route through Philistine territory. He explains His reasoning to Moses: "Lest the people change their minds when they see war and return to Egypt" (3:17). Although they don't understand, the Israelites follow God's unconventional route and experience hardships. But they also see God's supernatural provision.

The Israelites don't choose to go through the heart of the wilderness to Mount Sinai, but God guides them to a life of purpose and provides what they need to keep moving toward the Promised Land, one step at a time. On their own, they would have remained a nation enslaved and scorned.

But with God as their guide, they have provision and experience a transformational relationship with Him. Following God's route doesn't mean an easy fix, a hit of comfort, or a quick makeover. But it is an invitation to abandon their identity as slaves and live as His chosen nation.

God also wants to be our guide, even if that means taking us on paths we wouldn't choose. He offers us a promise and purpose that go above and beyond what this world offers. When our hearts are tied to an outcome or experience we design, we become consumers rather than cocreators with God as He intended. Paul tells the Corinthians, "We are God's fellow workers" (1 Corinthians 3:9). Redirecting our attention from our own problems and desires to focus instead on life in Christ, God works through us to bring blessings and solutions to a world that needs more than a surface fix.

In this partnership, we also consign to the understanding that God is the one who ultimately brings purpose and order. When we tie our purpose to something other than God or strive to create our own order, we wind up disappointed and dissatisfied. That's because God doesn't want to be our guide so He can secure power over us. He wants to partner with us. He also wants to love us as our Father. As we focus more on our relationship with Him and less on our changing circumstances, we tie our hearts to an unchanging hope that will satisfy us.

INVITATION

"If it seems too good to be true, it probably is." Has this been your experience too? Give an example. How is it helpful to remember this today?

DAILY BREAD

Read Romans 8:1–17. What does setting our minds on the flesh look like versus setting our minds on things of the Spirit? How might this transform our day-to-day experience?

SAY GRACE

Every good gift and every perfect gift is from above,
coming down from the Father of lights,
with whom there is no variation
or shadow due to change. (James 1:17)

Omni God

Mr. Lambert began our fifth-grade theology class by writing three terms on the chalkboard. He called these the "omnis" of God. The word *omni* made me think of a Hindu monk, cross-legged and clad in a saffron robe, chanting, "Ohmmm." I know now, of course, that the omni qualities of God and the Sanskrit word *om* are not to be confused. In Buddhist and Hindu meditation and yoga practice, the word *om*, also written *aum*, is a mantra that represents the whole world and all of its sounds. It acknowledges humanity's oneness with nature and all living things.

As Christians, however, we don't subscribe to equality but hierarchy, with God as the ultimate source of life—the Creator and Sustainer of the universe. Phew! I'm glad I'm not the one in charge of keeping the world spinning! Rather than trusting in Eastern religions' focus on self-enlightenment, we trust in God, who is the source of all enlightenment.

"Omni" is the Latin root for the word *all*. It is the first syllable of the three terms that were on the chalkboard that day. These terms describe the three unique attributes God reveals about Himself in the Bible.

Let's look at their meanings and some Bible verses that demonstrate how these qualities describe God.

Omniscience. God is all knowing. His knowledge is without limit. He knows everything in the past, present, and future. He knows our thoughts and every potential outcome. How do the following verses show God's omniscience?

Psalm 147:5 *His understanding has no limits*

1 John 3:20 *God is greater than our hearts and He knows everything*

Omnipresence. God is present everywhere at the same time. How do the following verses show God's omnipresence?

Jeremiah 23:24 *Can anyone hide in secret places? Says the Lord. Do not I fill heaven and earth?*

Proverbs 15:3 *The eyes of the Lord are everywhere, keeping an eye on the evil and the good.*

Omnipotence. God has unlimited power and potential. How do the following verses show God's omnipotence?

Matthew 19:26 *with God all things are possible*

Acts 26:8 *God raises the dead — (that is unlimited power!)*

The apostle Paul invites us to "be transformed by the renewal of your mind" (Romans 12:2). Again and again, God, in His Word, reminds us how huge He is. Inversely, we remember how small we are. In this place of humility, God renews our minds as we recognize our limited understanding and His unlimited wisdom and love for us, moving us to respond in obedience. The Bible uses the word *submission* to capture the importance of our obedience and humility:

Submission is "the action or fact of accepting or yielding to a superior force or the will or authority of another person."

How would you define the word *submission*?

What do you think it means to submit to God's authority?

God is God → Im not God

When Jesus teaches His disciples to pray, He begins the prayer with intimacy, "Our Father," and worship, "in heaven" (Matthew 6:9). Then Jesus tells the disciples they should petition God the Father according to His authority over us: "Your will be done" (6:10). Now I know "Your will" is just a couple of letters away from "my will." And if I'm honest, in my own prayers, I can be tempted to pray my own will or desires and then baptize it at the end with, "I ask all this in Your will. Amen."

We know Jesus is teaching the disciples to seek and pray for God's desired outcome. This means praying for His will and kingdom, not just our own desires and personal kingdoms. As Jesus' disciples, we know we can't always see how things should go from our vantage point. In our limited capacity, our own prayers might be too small. We pray the Lord's Prayer because God doesn't want us to rely on our own power but on His unlimited, all-loving, grace-giving, resurrecting power that doesn't just fix things temporarily—it makes all things new.

Submission isn't a feel-good word you'd see on a cute canvas on your wall. I don't think the local gift shop would sell a lot of wall signs stamped with the verse "Submit yourselves, then, to God" (James 4:7). Giving a necklace engraved with the word *submissive* to someone you love might not be well received. But for Christians who believe God is omniscient, omnipresent, and omnipotent, the word *submissive* defines Jesus' journey of perfect obedience to His Father's will, our journey with Jesus, and the Israelite's journey. "Your way, God, not my way" is the refrain we learn as Christians, trusting that His ways are higher.

> For as the heavens are higher than the earth, so are My ways higher than your ways and My thoughts than Your thoughts. (Isaiah 55:9)

We are infinitely less than God, and we don't need to hesitate to submit our imperfect will.

There is one more omni quality of God that I want us to look at: *omnibenevolent*. This one is up for debate among many monotheists. With all the sin and evil in the world, is God really the source of unlimited goodness? Christians have the answer. God is so good that He became "sin who knew no sin, so that in Him we might become the righteousness of God" (2 Corinthians 5:21). This verse takes my breath away because it assures us that our God *is* omnibenevolent.

Sit and receive and meditate on the promise of God's limitless power, wisdom, presence, and goodness. As we rest in the omnibenevolence of God, we trust that He knows our entire journey. God invites you to focus on this moment.

In the wilderness, the Israelites learned to live in the moment by receiving God's daily bread and to walk in His wisdom for their futures.

We, too, must soak in how big and capable God is, trust that He is good, relinquish our grip on control, and follow Him, praying with confidence, "Give us this day" (Matthew 6:11).

INVITATION

Which one of God's omni qualities gives you the most comfort in your wilderness seasons? Why?

omnipresent

Can you think of a time when you experienced this quality of God in your life? Describe it here:

How does this comfort you today?

DAILY BREAD

Read Ephesians 1:3–10. How does this passage demonstrate God's omni qualities? How does it speak to your life right now?

He predestined us to be adopted as his heirs - omnipresence, omnibenevolent, omnipotent omniscience -

SAY GRACE

I will give to the LORD the thanks due
to His righteousness, and I will sing praise
to the name of the LORD, the Most High. (Psalm 7:17)

WEEK 2: DAY 4

Do It Afraid

"Bloody Mary, Bloody Mary, Bloody Mary." As my mom held me in the dark bathroom in front of the mirror, she said the words, and I cowered and cried. She was trying to show me that nothing would happen. But I held onto my fear like a talisman. Earlier that week, a boy in fourth grade, two years older than me, had turned around in the seat in front of me on the school bus and loudly whispered, "If you say her name three times in the dark in front of a mirror, she'll show up and haunt you!" From that moment on, the fear was implanted, and I was terrified of being alone in the dark. Even though nothing happened when my mom said "Bloody Mary," I was still afraid. A shiver still runs down my spine from time to time when I'm alone in the dark with a mirror. Fear is like that. An involuntary reaction, sometimes illogical, can paralyze us and prevent us from recognizing the truth.

Fear and abandonment entered the world like unwelcome guests when Adam and Eve sampled the forbidden fruit. God looked for them in the Garden of Eden, and they hid in fear and shame. After the fall, sin entered and fertilized our hearts and stirred emotions that separate us from God. Fast-forward several thousand years to the shores of the Red Sea, where "the people of Israel lifted up their eyes, and behold, the Egyptians were marching after them, and they feared greatly" (Exodus 14:10). Egyptian armies are approaching on horseback and armed to the teeth. The Israelites are unarmed and on foot. The sea blocks their only escape. God's people need a solution, pronto.

From here, we witness two very different answers on how they should respond.

What is Moses' response in Exodus 14:13–14?

What is God's response in Exodus 14:15?

Moses' words are what we put on coffee mugs and greeting cards. But upon closer inspection, we see God redirects the Israelites. Instead of "standing firm," He tells them to "go forward."

The Israelites' human response is fear, but then God tells them to keep moving in faith toward His promise. I imagine Moses' hands shake as fear pulses through his veins, but he resolves to trust God. With determination, Moses lifts his staff and stretches out his hand. Of course, we know what happens after that. This scene makes me think of the slogan "Do it afraid." When we face a challenge to go forward—even if we feel yanked back by fear—we see two teams on opposing sides of the field. Satan and his minions are chanting lies, wanting nothing more than for us to be paralyzed in place. God and His angel armies are standing together in anticipation, clapping and rallying our faith and courage to keep going, even as fear makes our feet heavy and our minds noisy. God and His armies aren't just passive observers. They come to our aid even as fear threatens to have the last word.

Write It on Your Heart

Look up Isaiah 41:10.

Look up Psalm 91:11–12.

Fear has the power to isolate and incapacitate, blinding us from recognizing God's presence. Can you think of a time when fear has tempted you to hide or hold back? Give yourself grace as you recognize that fear can be a natural first response. But it doesn't have to have the final say. We can follow God with sweaty palms and gritted teeth, knowing that we never go alone.

Pray: Lord, sometimes when we step into holy ground, Your call to us feels like the scariest steps we have ever had to take. We pray for confidence and confirmation that we have heard Your direction and boldness and obedience to step forward in faith. Amen.

Is God prompting you to take steps forward in faith? We know God sometimes calls us to stand firm, but this story demonstrates that standing firm isn't always the answer. The litmus test is whether we are acting out of a place of fear or trust. Are we listening to Satan's whispers or to God's truth as He empowers us to step forward in faith even when the path appears impassable?

INVITATION

Think of a time when you "did it afraid." How did you "go forward," even though you felt doubt and fear? What was the blessing you saw through that experience?

How does that memory help you today?

DAILY BREAD

Look up Exodus 14:15–31. How does the Lord's response to Moses give you the confidence to move forward in faith today?

SAY GRACE

But I with the voice of thanksgiving
will sacrifice to You; what I have vowed I will pay.
Salvation belongs to the Lord! (Jonah 2:9)

A Better Sacrifice, A Better Guide

In Exodus 14:31, God acts as the Israelites' guide and guardian. As the Israelites step through the Red Sea onto dry land, God moves His pillar of cloud from in front of them to behind them, shielding them from the Egyptian army. Then God provides light to guide the Israelites forward and sends darkness to confuse the Egyptians.

God's activity in this account parallels His work in the first chapter of Genesis. He hovers over the deep of the waters (see 1:2), brings light in the darkness (see 1:3) and separates the water from dry land (see 1:9). God shows us His creative power in the creation account. In Exodus, His power is just as personal, palpable, and powerful. Through Moses, the Creator confronts Pharaoh's tyranny. And despite the Israelites' fear and hopelessness, God brings direction and protection, relaunching the Israelites as a nation of free men and women, no longer defined by the oppression and power of their enemy.

I want this account to be the "happily ever after" that my heart seems programmed for. But as you know, it is just the beginning of a long struggle. It is easy to see evil in an opponent, but it is trickier to recognize that the enemy also hides in plain sight in our own flesh.

> For I do not do what I want, but I do the very thing I hate. Now if I do what I do not want, I agree with the law, that it is good. So now it is no longer I who do it, but sin that dwells within me. (Romans 7:15–17)

God frees the Israelites from captivity in Egypt, but sin still binds them to their past as slaves.

God's journey with Israel points us to our need for Jesus as our Redeemer and Savior.

Another Path, Another Promise

We could frame the account of the Red Sea as God's ultimate victory, but we cannot deny that the drowned Egyptians, swept up on the shore, were also His workmanship; Pharaoh and Moses were raised in the same household. But before we get too worked up over the incongruity of the Old Testament Yahweh versus our New Testament Savior, Jesus, we must remember that our omniscient God takes all the time He needs to unfold His story of redemption. While God stood as a veil-like cloud to divide the Israelites from the attacking Egyptians (see Exodus 14:19), Jesus' death at the hands of His oppressors divided the veil that separated God from man.

In His resurrection, Jesus conquers the division that is death, bringing light and a path through darkness and chaos into the promise of eternal life. Just as God dwells among the Israelites, He sends His Son to dwell in human flesh. Jesus liberates humanity from the oppression of sin as God makes another path for His people to cross through. Ultimately, God wants to create a path for all people to reach the promised land of heaven—eternal life with Him.

The Israelites are freed from slavery in Egypt, but they are still slaves to sin. They need God to break spiritual chains that can only be accomplished through the blood of Christ, which is represented by the blood of sacrificial animals. The Book of Leviticus unpacks the concept of God's forgiveness coming from sacrifice. The people have to offer several substitutionary sacrifices like bulls, goats, lambs, and doves to atone for their sins. These sacrifices have to continue because the one sacrifice—Christ dying for our sins on the cross—has not yet come. Christ's blood makes animal sacrifices unnecessary. However, people continue to fall short of the Law given to Moses on Mount Sinai.

Write It on Your Heart

Look up Hebrews 10:11.

Jesus, God in flesh, also known as the Lamb of God, is the only one who can fulfill the Law, making Him the perfect (and final) sacrifice for all people.

Look up Hebrews 10:12.

Jesus' atonement cancels the need for God to remain separated from the people behind a veil in the Holy Place, which is where God dwells in the tabernacle. He instructs Moses to build the tabernacle as a shadow of God's true tabernacle in heaven. The tabernacle in the wilderness was not intended to be God's ultimate dwelling place. By Jesus' sacrifice and resurrection, God makes His dwelling place in each of us, through His Holy Spirit.

The happy ending is still coming, yet we have good news to share that changes everything. The great "I AM" lives within us through the Holy Spirit, meaning God's power goes before us and dwells within us. Our sin made us enemies of God. We were lost in darkness and confusion, but now we are resurrected people who bear the light of Jesus.

For by a single offering He has perfected for all time those who are being sanctified. And the Holy Spirit also bears witness to us; for after saying, "This is the covenant that I will make with them after those days, declares the Lord: I will put My laws on their hearts, and write them on their minds," then He adds, "I will remember their sins and their lawless deeds no more." (Hebrews 10:14–17)

INVITATION

How is the Holy Spirit your guide today?

DAILY BREAD

Look up Romans 6:5–6. Just as God gives the Israelites a new identity, how does He give us a new identity in Christ?

SAY GRACE

The Lord has promised good to me,
His Word my hope secures;
He will my shield and portion be
As long as life endures. (*LSB* 744:2)

WEEK 3

The Provision of Praise

The LORD is my strength
and my song, and He has become
my salvation; this is my God,
and I will praise Him.

Exodus 15:2

———

How We Worship

The word *worship* finds its etymology in the Old English word *worth-ship,* which refers to something worthy. Worship is a way we position our hearts toward God, remembering that He is number one in our lives. Martin Luther puts it well when he recognizes,

> We cannot give God anything; for everything is already His, and all we have comes from Him. We can only give Him praise, thanks, and honor.[2]

"Praise, thanks, and honor" capture the essence of a worshipful response to God, but what is worship exactly? A Google search led me to many different views of worship. A narrow definition might speak only of our time worshiping together as a church body, but I think worship starts with our mindset and the state of our hearts and informs our everyday lives.

Spirit and Truth

Jesus tells the woman at the well that "true worshipers will worship the Father in spirit and in truth" (John 4:23), pointing us to the importance of the Gospel and the Holy Spirit, who inspires and fuels our faith. While the Good News of Jesus is unchanging, over the centuries and especially today, there is much debate about Christian worship styles, formats, and protocols. Should we bang drums? clap hands? listen to praise songs sung from a stage or hymns from a choir in a choir loft?

The Israelite women, led by Miriam, dance and shake tambourines during the first worship song recorded in the Bible after the Israelites cross the Red Sea (see Exodus 15:20). But that's not the formula we have to follow. The throne room of heaven will have "every nation, from all tribes and peoples and languages," meaning worship in heaven will be a diverse display of adoration for God (Revelation 7:9).

Worshiping as a congregation is a powerful and vital function of the Body of Christ, whether with hymns and an organ or worship songs and an electric guitar. God also calls us to a life of worship outside the walls of the church building. Worship, for me, happens with my hands raised in church; it also happens as I pray and pour out my heart to God while I drive for school pickup. Worship happens when I scribble poetry and when my daughter dances to "Hosanna" blasting from our smart speaker. Worship happens in a mother's coos as she cradles gratitude in her heart, wondering over her beautiful child made in God's image. Worship happens when friends swap stories of God's goodness between sips of coffee.

We worship God when we echo the question of the Israelites: "Who is like You, O LORD, among the gods?" (Exodus 15:11).

Write It on Your Heart

Look up Exodus 15:11. *who among the gods is like you, O Lord? who is like you — majestic in holiness, awesome in glory working wonders*

The function of worship is to remember and revere our heavenly Father, to praise and glorify Him for His good gifts to us. We remember that God is at the center of all things, joins all things together, and has a purpose in all things. Our default setting is self-focused, but worship acknowledges that God is greater and we are less. In times of waiting and uncertainty, acknowledging that God is still good and in control recalibrates our hearts to see God's blessings in the wilderness and our desperate moments as opportunities to see how God provides what we truly need.

Pray: Lord, as we worship You throughout our day, may the lifting of our hands show our joy that You abide with us always. We ask that You would give us eyes to see Your mighty works, and when we are tempted to give in to despair, remind us of the victory we have in You. Amen.

We reach the end of our human ability when we try to mine the depths of science, psychology, and philosophy. When we try to mine the depths of our souls, we come face-to-face with our mortality and are left wanting answers and meaning. Worship is surrendering to God, who is so vast that we are left only with trust. Even when we don't have all the answers, God is always good.

INVITATION

Describe what worship looks like in your church or the service you prefer. *traditional*

Why is this your preferred style of worship?
more reverent + focussed

How do you worship God outside of church?
always thankful in nature + see God's power in things around me.

DAILY BREAD

Look up Exodus 15:1–7. Notice that the Israelites sing about their personal experience with God in their lives and what they had witnessed. If you were to sing a song of praise to God for what He is doing in your life today, what might it include?

SAY GRACE

For from Him and through Him and
to Him are all things. To Him be
glory forever. Amen. (Romans 11:36)

WEEK 3: DAY 2

The Sacrifice of Praise

"I was in an accident. The car is totaled." The meaning of his words hit me in waves. He had been in an accident—but he was okay; he had to be since he was delivering the news to me in a calm but clearly shaken voice. Phone service was spotty, but he conveyed the location of the accident—only a couple miles from my parents' house across rain-soaked and winding roads. My dad rushed to the scene, and I waited at home, listening to the rain's percussion and praying. Finally, from the window, I saw my husband, Nathan, who was soaking wet. He walked as if in a funeral procession toward the door, bearing what remained: the rearview mirror and his soaked Bible.

The gravity of what happened hit me the same time overwhelming gratitude did. "Thank You, Lord!" I shouted. When Nathan came through the door, I wrapped my arms around him and spoke into his shoulder, "Praise God you are okay!" At that moment, words of praise spilled from my lips easily. God had protected my husband, who stood whole and unharmed before me.

On the other side of the Red Sea, on the other side of slavery, the Israelites worship God for His great deliverance. Exodus 15 records the first song of praise in the Bible. There are only a few details about this scene, but they paint a vibrant picture of joy, celebration, and liberation. Imagine 600,000 men singing together with their wives and children as the women dance with tambourines.

The Egyptian culture they left behind was known for its many gods.

There was a god of war and hunting, a god of wisdom, and a sun god that brought light. Even Pharaoh was believed to be a god.

The Israelites worship only Yahweh. Despite the Egyptians' wealth and strong army, despite the many gods they worship, it is Yahweh, the God of Israel, who displays His awesome strength and delivers the Israelites. Israel erupts in spontaneous praise, expressing its joy and relief as it recognizes this truth.

Have you ever burst into praise in response to God's miraculous hand in your own circumstances? In moments of relief and gratitude, praise and thanksgiving to God come as easily as breathing. But praise to God does not always flow naturally and continually in our everyday experiences, despite Scripture emphasizing its importance in the life of a Christian. When life is routine and one day is much like the last, we can get swept up in our realities and priorities and overlook God. When life is hard, when the car is wrecked, and when it's raining and dark, we might be desperately waiting for God to respond to our struggle. Perhaps we haven't yet seen the praiseworthy breakthrough. The author of Hebrews recognizes that sometimes praising God in wilderness seasons is an act of obedience.

Look up Hebrews 13:15. How would you explain this verse in your own words? *Through Jesus let us continually offer to God a sacrifice of praise — I confess His name. — In all things give the Lord praise*

This verse emphasizes the need for worship in everyday life, especially in wilderness seasons. The Greek word for *continually* in verse 15 is translated as "through it all." Wait a minute. Does "through it all" mean I should praise God when I spill my coffee all over myself as I get into the car? when my car breaks down? when my sister is diagnosed with cancer? when I lose someone I thought I could never live without? "Through it all" challenges me to consider how praising God in impossible circumstances is an act of worship.

The Fruit of Praise in Difficult Circumstances

We can witness this reality in the life of Paul, who sings praises to God in jail, or Stephen, who is full of the Holy Spirit while he is on trial. We can look at Jesus' words, which continually point to His Father despite the wicked world He lives in. We can look to Jesus, who submits to suffering on the cross, which puts an end to the old system of sacrifice and offering. Through Jesus, our praise and prayer become the new incense and sacrifice that pleases our Father. I remember the hidden reality of God's kingdom, which inspires me to give thanks amid the ache of not yet. Christ crucified and Christ resurrected transform our present reality, even in suffering. There is nothing we can add to the work Jesus did on our behalf on the cross, but our words are a pleasing sacrifice and good fruit to God as we praise Him in gratitude, obedience, and worship.

This gives me hope as I am reminded that there are blessings when we push through the doubt, fatigue, and malaise that threaten to define our outlook and as we choose to speak words that profess the faith we have in Jesus.

We worship in moments of joy and awe, under twinkling stars, overlooking canyons, lost in the hymn of a chorus of voices in church. We also worship in our everyday lives when we're aching tired, the laundry is overflowing, and the bathroom needs to be cleaned. We worship in the wilderness when our grief and doubt feel like a mountain that won't move. Our worship is a sacrifice of praise with our lips as we remind ourselves and others of the reality that Jesus won for us on the cross. Our praise in hopeless circumstances testifies to a victorious kingdom in a fallen world.

God is worthy of praise when we see His mighty hand split seas and protect our loved ones. As Christians, we are also challenged to recognize God, who is worthy of praise, even as we sit with Job in dust and ashes and proclaim, "And after my skin has been thus destroyed, yet in my flesh I shall see God" (Job 19:26).

INVITATION

Can you remember when you thanked and worshiped God for doing something miraculous in your life?

Can you describe a time when you worshiped God even though you didn't get what you prayed for? Contrast these two experiences. *death of a parent, or close relative, loss of hearing for a grandchild*

DAILY BREAD

Look up Acts 16:20–26. Consider the circumstances Paul and Silas are in as they praise God. How does their posture of worship toward God in hard circumstances inspire you during your season? *they were praying & singing after having been beaten, put in prison & shackled*

SAY GRACE

When darkness veils His lovely face,
I rest on His unchanging grace;
In ev'ry high and stormy gale
My anchor holds within the veil. (*LSB* 576:2)

On Christ the solid rock I stand all other ground is sinking sand.

WEEK 3: DAY 3

Is He Worthy?

Social media and I have had a toxic relationship. It's where I promote my work and share what God is putting on my heart, but it can easily become an altar where I worship to seek validation. Did someone like what I posted? Did they *love* it? Did they share my blog post or comment on it?

Early in my career, if I wasn't intentional, I would fall into the trap of checking and rechecking my posts for responses. A positive response would buoy my mood, and when I didn't get the likes, shares, or comments I hoped for, I would become anxious and question my worth. I've had trouble finding a healthy balance with social media. But I've learned to hold social media loosely and use it in healthier ways.

We all worship something. As I mentioned earlier, worship derives from the Old English word *worth-ship*, meaning we worship anything we give priority and value in our lives. It is more comfortable to say, "Well, of course, I worship God first," but let's consider how our actual lives align with the things we value. It was easy to say that I didn't have a problem prioritizing God over social media, but when I installed an app that tracked my usage, the reality challenged me to reconsider.

Our journey in the wilderness challenges us to reprioritize the things we've welcomed into the luggage of our lives. In seasons of change and uncertainty, we can let go of the things weighing us down—habits, unhelpful beliefs, codependent relationships, addictions—or we can let them define us. We learn to reevaluate the things we're holding onto as we clutch the things that matter more closely. Worship helps us redefine our priorities and recenter our hearts on God's truth, which gives a new perspective on our struggle and a new purpose to our journey. Our lives reflect our priorities in different ways. A few priorities are listed below, along with space to jot down any thoughts that bubble to the surface as you consider them.

① **Time is a concrete measurement.** Ponder where you invest your time and why. Are you spending time praying? Are you in God's Word? Are you growing in faith with other believers? This week, pay attention to where you spend your time and consider how this aligns with your values.

③ **Money is also concrete.** An honest look at our budget gives us a snapshot of our priorities. Are you spending or contributing dollars to things that matter to you? to God? Do you need to take a closer look at the amount you're spending on Amazon or Starbucks (the struggle is real!)? Ask God to help you align your budget with the things He values.

② **Words have power.** Whose words hold the most value in your life? No word is weightier than Jesus' words for our lives, yet it is tempting to steep ourselves in other books, podcasts, opinions, and newsfeeds that consequently inform how we act and think. Ask God to help you take in His Word as sustenance and spit out the words in your life that don't have value.

There are other areas we can look at more closely, but if we do it all at once, we can quickly become overwhelmed and defeated. This is a process of living in God's grace and responding to His gentle nudges to realign our lives with the truth of His Word. Know that God loves you and gave His Son to save you and make you His own.

I love those who love Me, and those who seek Me diligently find Me. (Proverbs 8:17)

Ask someone you trust to share what they think your values and priorities are. This honest conversation can give you a fresh perspective on how you are living out your faith. Record additional thoughts or discoveries below.

INVITATION

Is God inviting you to look more closely at an area of your life? What's one measurable step you could take toward making a change in that area?

DAILY BREAD

Look up Deuteronomy 6:1–8. What does it mean to love the Lord your God with all your heart and with all your soul and with all your might? How does it apply to your life right now?

It should surround us –
- should be upon our hearts
- taught to our children
- talk about them as you go about your day or sit down, when you lie down + get up – 1st/last things of the day
- tie them to your foreheads
- symbols on your hands
- write them on your door frames
{ All-encompassing your life }

Look up John 10:10. What is the abundance John refers to?

Everlasting Life

*"The thief comes only to steal
+ kill + destroy; I have come that
they may have life and have it
to the full.*

SAY GRACE

For where your treasure is,
there your heart will be also.

(Matthew 6:21)

WEEK 3: DAY 4

The Fruit of Praise

On day three of this week, we had a bit of a challenging exercise, right? But I think you would agree that God challenges us to grow.

Today's culture tries to soften God's judgment to make Him more appealing. Still, the Christian life can entail painful self-evaluation, self-sacrifice, and coming face-to-face with God, who is far holier, more just, more powerful, and more righteous than we can fathom. The result of this kind of encounter is, well, uncomfortable. We sinful humans are all about what's easy, convenient, comfortable, and customizable. We cut and carve and push and squeeze God into our man-made molds to meet our spiritual needs. However, the God of the Bible shames the strong and wise; He offends the mind and cracks open the heart. He draws us out of our bunkers of self-preservation and pride to live lives devoted to loving and serving others.

Write It on Your Heart

Look up Galatians 5:13. *Do not use your freedom to indulge the sinful nature rather serve one another in love. Liberty is not license but freedom to serve God & each other in love*

Objects of His Mercy

The God of the Old Testament is especially challenging for us to understand in our modern world. In his song of worship in Exodus 15, Moses paints a picture of God as a warrior with burning anger, blasting nostrils, and a puff of breath that moves the sea as His weapon of war. In contrast, I can get caught up in our culture's image of an easygoing, happy-go-lucky God, kind of like a Bob Ross in the sky, painting happy trees into creation! God *is* gracious, happy, and creative, but we can't limit Him to the emotions and characteristics that keep us comfortable. If we made God in our own image, He would be stripped of His divinity, which makes Him elevated, holy, and transformational. Scottish evangelist and author Oswald Chambers speaks to this:

> When we preach the love of God there is a danger of forgetting that the Bible reveals not first the love of God but the intense, blazing holiness of God, with His love at the center of that holiness.[3]

If we make God in our image, then we wouldn't have a God who provokes us to change. True worship of God leads to transformation. It is unavoidable. When we worship God and accept that He is beyond our comprehension, we cannot help but be humbled, softened, convicted, and changed. As vessels in the potter's hand, we surrender to God's fire, which softens, reshapes, and makes us His masterpiece. The process may be humbling, disorienting, or even painful, but in His grip, we know His love.

Spirit come, make my heart Your home
Spirit melt me, take my heart of stone
Spirit mold me, into what You can use
Spirit fill me, with Your message of truth
Spirit send me, to share the Good News.[4]

God, in blazing holiness, comes in humility as Jesus meets us as we are and shows us who He wants us to become. He loves us too much to leave us as we are. The first question God asks in the Bible is addressed to Adam and Eve: "Where are you?" (Genesis 3:9). And daily, He comes to us with the same question: "Where are you, My child?" God, who is more holy than we can comprehend, comes to us where we are and clothes us to be righteous before Him. The God of the universe invites us into His throne room, not as a servant but as His beloved child.

INVITATION

How have you fallen into the trap of making God in your own image?

How does God restore your perspective?

DAILY BREAD

Look up Exodus 15:7–11. Does this description of God challenge your understanding of Him? Why or why not?

Look up Romans 9:19–26. How would you explain these verses?

Don't question God - He is God I am not. He does all this to share His riches (Heaven) with believers

How is God sovereign, even in the wilderness?

SAY GRACE

You make known to me the path of life;
in Your presence there is fullness of joy;
at Your right hand are pleasures forevermore. (Psalm 16:11)

WEEK 3: DAY 5

Promise Keeper

At just six months old, our son became attached to a Christian song-book, with buttons that played the melody of well-loved tunes. It quickly became a routine to sing the songs before bed. Our son is now two years old. The book is taped together and out of batteries, but he still loves hearing us sing the songs to him every night.

One night, I forgot to sing when Daddy was gone. I've learned that breaking routines with toddlers is a very serious offense! He kept repeating, "Jesus! Bible! Jesus! Bible!" Delighted and confused, I went about the process of interpreting toddler language. Then, I realized he was trying to get me to sing his songs. His favorite goes like this: "Jesus loves me! This I know, for the Bible tells me so" (*LSB* 588:1). For some, this is the only Christian song they remember from their childhood. The words are simple but profound! I didn't realize until that moment the powerful seeds we were planting in his heart through the repetition of our bedtime medley.

The Israelites used songs to teach, remember, and pass on the stories of how God touched and shaped them. Throughout the Old Testament, God reminds His people to *remember*. The traditions and holidays of the Jewish people helped them remember the bigger story they were part of—some that we still participate in today. The Sabbath Day was set aside by God in the beginning for us to remember Him. The Israelites used names and built altars to remember God's presence and provision in their lives. For instance, Abraham remembered God's provision of a ram in the place of his son as a sacrifice, naming the place of his offering Yahweh *yireh,* meaning "The LORD will provide" (Genesis 22:14).

God's people remember what He has done for them and that they are chosen by God, redeemed by God, and part of a bigger story that is being written to glorify God. Through Jesus, we are grafted into this story. After the Israelites cross the Red Sea, the first song of praise they sing is a fore-taste of the great celebration and praises that will be sung when we are free from the oppression of sin (see Revelation 5).

The song of the sea is a beautiful snapshot of worship and storytelling. The Israelites use the power of song to store the work of God's miraculous hand in their hearts. Of course, we know that it doesn't take long for them to shift from praise to self-pity as they face their utter reliance on God in the wilderness. But their song weaves this great event into their collective memory and the identity of their descendants. It is also preserved for us to hear and hold on to today, even in our own wilderness seasons.

Provision Today, Promises for Tomorrow

In the day-to-day grind, our bodies continually remind us of our human frailty and need for the Savior. We hunger and thirst, shiver and sweat; our bodies ache for sleep. And as we get older, our bodies ache for relief! A friend recently joked, "If we spend most of our money on food and clothes, then why are we still hungry and complain we have nothing to wear?" We have a greater need, but it can't be met with money, food, clothes, or anything else this world can offer. God built us to need Him and rely on Him day by day with every bite, sip, and snore. But rather than letting our momentary needs consume us, God points us to a rhythm of reliance, rest, and worship. We can pause and sing a song of praise as we remember the trials God has brought us through and as we look to God's ultimate provision in Jesus. Praise and worship bring our hearts back to Jesus in this now-and-not-yet world. We remember what He has done, which inspires faith in what He will do. We find provision in "the oil of gladness instead of mourning, the garment of praise instead of a faint spirit" (Isaiah 61:3).

Like the Israelites, we worship God for all the ways He has provided and look to how He will continue to provide.

The people closed the song by anticipating how God would defeat their enemies as they entered the Promised Land.

Write It on Your Heart

Look up Exodus 15:14–15. *The nations will hear + tremble, anguish will grip the people of Philistia. The chiefs of Edom will be terrified, the leaders of Moab will be seized with trembling, the people of Canaan will melt away.*

The Holy Spirit strengthens the Israelites' trust in the Lord as they worship Him, learning He is able. They don't know how and definitely don't know how long it will take (it is probably for the best that way). If they had held tightly to God's promise, they would have left the wilderness and begun to take possession of the Promised Land eleven days after leaving Mount Sinai (see Deuteronomy 1:2). Instead, they listen to ten unfaithful spies (see Numbers 13:25–33). Distrusting God, they seek a leader to take them back to Egypt. As punishment, they have to wander in the wilderness for forty years. Aside from Joshua and Caleb, the two faithful spies, that whole generation dies in the wilderness. But forty years later, the Israelites get to see their praise become a reality. We read in Joshua, "Not one word of all the good promises that the LORD had made to the house of Israel had failed; all came to pass" (Joshua 21:45). For us, the wilderness leads to the promised land of heaven, whether the promises are fulfilled on this side of a temporary struggle or on the other side of God's ultimate promise of eternal life.

As I get older, I'm learning I need my imagination more than ever. When this world feels heavy, I picture the world as it will be when Christ returns: flowers don't wilt and die, bodies don't grow old; there is no pain, suffering, and depression; relationships aren't strained, and hearts aren't broken. Picture a world where we only experience the best things life has to offer. Instead of looking at the sky to find pictures in clouds, my kids and I paint pictures of what we think eternal life with Jesus will look like. If you haven't spent time considering this, I challenge you to. This is our promised land and inheritance. Just as God kept His promises to the Israelites,

He will keep His promises to us.

> For behold, I create new heavens and a new earth, and the former things shall not be remembered or come into mind. (Isaiah 65:17)

Worship helps us take a break from the distractions that dominate our attention. Worship helps us focus our attention on God's reality that is now, as His kingdom touches our broken world, as well as not yet, as we cling to the promise of what Christ will do when He returns.

INVITATION

As you face doubt and unmet needs in the wilderness, how does God renew your faith each day? How does He give you hope for a future? *A new day – a beautiful sunrise, — just knowing God is Lord of all today as He was yesterday.*

DAILY BREAD

Look up Exodus 15:12–19. Notice how the Israelites began to anticipate what God would do in the song. How do we do this in our Christian songs and hymns today?

SAY GRACE

Therefore let us be grateful for
receiving a kingdom that
cannot be shaken, and thus let
us offer to God acceptable worship,
with reverence and awe. (Hebrews 12:28)

WEEK 4

Bittersweet Blessing

When they came to Marah,
they could not drink the water
of Marah because it was bitter.

Exodus 15:23

———

Shepherded

I used to own a business that provided hair and makeup services for brides. That experience taught me that there's nothing like a wedding to cause a lot of stir. For some of these brides, it was as if their whole lives were leading up to this paramount moment. As a newlywed at the time, I couldn't help but wonder if they'd considered what married life would be like after their big day. Did they know they'd have to figure out meal planning, get a joint bank account, and remember to put the cans out on garbage day?

As the Israelites take in God's overwhelming miracle of parting the Red Sea, they are also on the cusp of experiencing the struggles of everyday life in the wilderness. Their bodies are buzzing with adrenaline and anticipation at God's miraculous display. Then they look out over a vast desert and realize their new lives are only just beginning.

Moses made Israel set out from the Red Sea, and they went into the wilderness of Shur. (Exodus 15:22)

The word *made* in this verse strikes me, so I did a little more investigation and found that it comes from the Hebrew word *nasa. Nasa* means "to pull up, set out, or journey." We need to understand that setting out on a journey with this many people was no easy feat. It's hard enough to get my family of five going on a road trip. Socks fly. Shoes are tugged on haphazardly as travel coffee mugs spill and the dog tries to escape. You get the picture. Let's multiply this by hundreds of thousands of families; we can imagine it was quite the production. Not only was it a great amount of work, but the Israelites were reluctant to set out. While they had seen God show up in big ways throughout their captivity in Egypt and escaped from it, they would be entering a new season of unknowns.

The great exodus from Egypt was behind them. In a way, they were like newlyweds learning a new rhythm of trust and reliance on God for their ordinary yet essential needs. Departing the familiarity of Egypt was bitter-sweet, exhilarating, and terrifying. They know they don't have the supplies they need to cross the desert with their own resources and strength, yet their passage through the Red Sea proves that God could provide for them. Moses gives them the push they need to take the next step in faith toward the challenges ahead.

Our lives are dotted with inevitable and difficult transitions—college, marriage, a new baby, a new job, retirement, moving, experiencing illness, or losing someone we love. Some are welcomed, sweet, and exciting (scary nonetheless), and some are bitter, hard, and unwanted. Whether the change is happening by our own decision or thrust upon us, we set out unprepared and look to God to provide what we'll need to make it through. For the Is-raelites, life will get harder before it gets better. They will be stretched to the end of their human capacity, even going three days without water. Yet the God of compassion is with them, providing what they desperately need. The Israelites' story is recorded for us to learn from and be encouraged by God, our provider, even when we feel stretched to our limits. By faith, we move forward, step by step, trusting that God will give us the physical and spiritual things we need today and every day: forgiveness, grace, mercy, a friend to listen to us, a nap, or momentary relief. The Israelites' lives, and ours, are never out of His careful watch or provision.

Green-Pasture God

I read the other day that a shepherd smells like his sheep. Since a shep-herd sleeps with his sheep, this makes sense. But when I read it, it surprised and encouraged me. After all, Jesus calls Himself our Good Shepherd.

Write It on Your Heart

Look up John 10:27–28.

My sheep listen to my voice; I know them, and they follow me. I give them eternal life and they shall never perish, no one can snatch them out of my hand.

Jesus isn't afraid to lay down in the dirt and grime with us. He doesn't ask us to go places He hasn't already gone or to make a bigger sacrifice than He has already made. As Jesus leads us through the wilderness, we learn to trust Him to know our suffering and provide the comfort and provision we need. As we launch out into the unknown, we trust that God knows the way and the means. He invites us to take the next step of obedience as we repent and believe His Good News is for us.

> The LORD is my shepherd; I shall not want.
> He makes me lie down in green pastures.
> He leads me beside still waters.
> He restores my soul.
> He leads me in paths of righteousness
> for His name's sake. (Psalm 23:1–3)

INVITATION

What kind of season are you in right now? How is God challenging you to rely on Him more? *aging, body aches, trust God for relief + physical strength*

DAILY BREAD

Look up Exodus 15:22–24. Have you ever been desperate for God to provide something you needed? *Healing for a family member*

Can you imagine how the Israelites feel when the water they need turns out to be bitter? How would you respond in their circumstances? *the same – grumble*

SAY GRACE

And whatever you do, in word or deed, do everything
in the name of the Lord Jesus, giving thanks
to God the Father through Him. (Colossians 3:17)

Now and Not Yet

Three days earlier, the Israelites had been celebrating. Then, they start grumbling. After they leave the Red Sea and enter the wilderness of Shur, they wander for three days and can't find water. When they finally discover a well, they find they cannot drink from it because the water is bitter. They had watched God divide and congeal water into walls, but now they are afraid they will die of thirst! Their experience is bittersweet—a bitter struggle for survival contrasted against the sweetness of God's astounding wonders and provision. I can imagine them asking, "Why, God?! Why did You bother to save us from the brutal treatment of the Egyptians only to let us suffer in the wilderness?"

To a lesser degree, the word *bittersweet* describes our own lives. While we can't relate to the Israelites' circumstances, we can understand a life filled with setbacks and disillusionment juxtaposed against awe and beauty.

Bittersweet. What flavors and experiences does the word provoke? Bitterness can take you by surprise, causing a shudder through your entire body. It may make you think about a person, an unfair situation, or an unpleasant circumstance. Sweet, on the other hand, might bring to mind a moment of relaxation, a tender time with someone you love, or an unexpected blessing that came at an opportune time. There is a reason these two words are married into one—so interconnected that it is hard to decipher where one begins and the other ends. The word *bittersweet* describes how our difficult and painful experiences intertwine with life's blessings and beauty, like God's sweet manna kissing our bitter hunger. In these bare places, we face our deepest spiritual needs. We thirst for water the world can't supply.

Pray: Father, we pray for the living water of Your Holy Spirit. We pray for the Holy Spirit's friendship and comfort as we walk through this broken world. May we have spiritual eyes to see Your kingdom when our hearts grow faint and find continuous sustenance in Your Word and Sacraments. In Jesus' name. Amen.

The Cross Satisfies

After three desperate days, the Israelites find a well, but the water is bitter and undrinkable. It can only be made clean by God's healing, which comes when Moses throws a log into the water (see Exodus 15:25).

Write It on Your Heart

Look up Exodus 15:25. *Moses cried out to the Lord & the Lord showed him a piece of wood. He threw it into the water & it became sweet. The Lord tested them.*

The log can point to the cross that was planted in the ground to display God's bittersweet sacrifice. On our own, we cannot transform our circumstances, our relationships, or our hearts. When we look up, we see Jesus, who brought heaven down to us. Through all the bitterness, anger, insult, and torture the world hurls at God's Son, Satan's worst cannot destroy God's best for us. Life with Jesus means we don't deny or hide from suffering, struggles, or weakness. Instead, we recognize it as the path to transformation and, ultimately, restoration.

Martin Luther explained this state as the tension for us believers in God's kingdom that is now but has not fully come. As Christians, we are wanderers looking forward to the day when all God's promises will be fulfilled.

> We are continually going forth from Egypt through the desert, that is, through the way of cross and suffering to the Land of

Promise. We have been redeemed, and we are being redeemed continually. We have received adoption and are still receiving it.[5] *Luther*

Life on earth means navigating bitter wilderness paths while sipping the sweet water from the altar that sustains our lives right now. We are God's sons and daughters, yet foreigners in this world. We pray that God will provide healing today, and we trust that we will one day be completely healed and whole. We ask for daily bread and await a banquet feast. We sing "now and not yet" in the bittersweet tension between God's kingdom and a world that is a pale comparison to what is to come.

Life often leaves us unsatisfied, but we have faith, which is "the assurance of things hoped for, the conviction of things not seen" (Hebrews 11:1).

CUP BONE DRY

Lips cracked
a n d s i l e nt,
Eyes roll up to God,
Who isn't quiet
HIS BREATH makes us come alive,
HIS WORD—Water that revives,
A branch of tree makes bitter—sweet,
A tree, made cross, appears defeat,
An empty tomb
means no more death
T h i r s t y s o u l s
finally quenched
"Now and Not Yet,"
o u r battle cry
THE CROSS ASSURES
G O D 'S VICTORY[6]

INVITATION

When do you find it difficult to trust God's good provision amid this broken life?

Where do you want to see God's kingdom break through? How can you pray?

DAILY BREAD

Look up 1 John 3:2–3. How do these verses talk about the "now and not yet" in our lives as believers? *Dear friends, now we are children of God and what we will be has not yet been made known. But we know that when he appears we shall be like Him ... Everyone who has this hope in him purifies himself, just as He is pure*

SAY GRACE

What God ordains is always good:
Though I the cup am drinking
Which savors now of bitterness,
I take it without shrinking.
For after grief God gives relief,
My heart with comfort filling
And all my sorrow stilling. (*LSB* 760:5)

WEEK 4: DAY 3

The Bitter Root

"When the going gets tough, the tough get . . . grumbling?" That appears to be the go-to response for the Israelites. Of course, the rest of the saying is "the tough get going." But there is nowhere for the Israelites to go. They appear to be at the end of the line. Thirsty, weary from walking and carrying their possessions, and frightened, they blame Moses and God. Rather than take the present circumstances at face value, Moses is humble enough to recognize that God is the one with the solution. That's why when "the going gets tough," Moses gets praying. *am I humble enuf?*

Let's take a closer look at the story. As we read on day two of this week, the Israelites discover that the well they find after three days without water is full of bitter water. In the face of that disappointment and struggle, their hearts turn inward and they grumble bitterly. Moses, on the other hand, cries out to God for help. He doesn't have the answer, but he knows who does. In response to Moses' prayer, God instructs or shows him a log that will fix the problem. The Hebrew word used in Exodus 15:25 for *instructed* is related to a word you may find familiar: *torah*. *Torah* is the law or instruction God gave Moses on Mount Sinai.

When I read this story initially, I focused on the bitter well and the log, but this Hebrew word, *torah*, invites me to peel back the top layer of the text for a deeper meaning. Yes, God heals the water so the people can drink it. He also points to a deeper lesson the Israelites need to learn. God doesn't want their hearts to become stubborn and bitter. When they trust God and rely on Him, their hearts remain soft and open to His guidance.

Write It on Your Heart

Look up Proverbs 4:20–22.

*Pay attention to my words
Do not let them out of your heart
for they are life to those who find them &
health a whole man's body.*

God isn't just thinking about the Israelites' needs in that moment; He is focused on their transformation. Moses is "torah-ed" in the ultimate solution to the Israelites' thirst and bitterness of heart.

Bitterness has a dual meaning:

1. A sharp, pungent taste or smell

2. Anger, hurt, or resentment because of one's bad experiences or unjust treatment

What thoughts bubble up when you consider the word *bitterness*?

While the bitter water presents an imminent problem for the Israelites, we know that their bitterness toward God is the problem that will cost them forty years in the desert. God longs to instruct and help them reach the Promised Land in His timing and by His provision. He longs for them to look to Him. He longs for us to do so as well.

A failed marriage, a job loss, an injury, medical bills, an obstinate teenager, an aging parent, and many more things can cause us to become bitter. For me, even small things like heavy traffic, a surprise bill, a headache, or forgetting to buy milk can distract me from the goodness in my life and tempt me to grumble. These struggles are inevitable, and I don't think God expects us to be like Pollyannas, blindly optimistic and cheerful in the face of every difficulty. He created us with emotions to process our world and experiences. It isn't helpful to put Moses in one light as always peaceful and trusting either. Moses struggled with the same doubt, fear, and fatigue as the others; the difference is how he chose to respond.

Let's take another look:

[The Israelites] could not drink the water of Marah because it was bitter; therefore, it was named Marah. *And the people grumbled against Moses*, saying, "What shall we drink?" *And [Moses] cried to the* LORD. (Exodus 15:23–25, emphasis mine)

We can respond to struggle by becoming bitter and blaming circumstances, people around us, or God. Or we can cry to God for wisdom and perspective to move forward in faith. God continually instructs Moses to operate with a God-spective rather than through his limited human lens. Moses was discipled by God to be a humble leader. In fact, the Bible says Moses was the humblest man on earth (see Numbers 12:3). From that humility, Moses grows in trust and relationship with God, not just receiving His torah-instruction "on tablets of stone" but written on his heart as he looks to the future freedom that God promises.

INVITATION

What experiences have caused you to become bitter?

not given help when needed, being told how to do something I've done many times before

Has there been a time when you've expected others to know your needs or wants without asking? *yes, at home — around the house.*

How is God inviting you to respond differently in faith?

teaching me patience

DAILY BREAD

Look up Exodus 15:24–27. How have you experienced God as a healer? *If you listen carefully to the voice of the Lord your God and do what is right in His eyes, if you pay attention in all His decrees... "I am the Lord who heals you."*

SAY GRACE

Continue steadfastly in prayer,
being watchful in it with thanksgiving.
(Colossians 4:2)

WEEK 4: DAY 4

Heart Healing

Sin is part and parcel of our lives. We must endure the bitterness of a fallen world. The problem is amplified, the prophet Isaiah warns, when we allow sin to blind us from the truth, calling "evil good and good evil," mistaking "darkness for light" or "bitter for sweet." I want to sidestep these verses, believing I know the difference as I think, *Nope, not me. I wouldn't be the kind of person who confuses evil for good.* But Isaiah continues, explaining that the problem stems from "those who are wise in their own eyes, and shrewd in their own sight!" (Isaiah 5:19–22).

From the beginning, God has invited us to look to Him for wisdom and discernment about what is good. Adam and Eve didn't even know what evil was, but God gave them a choice: "Will you trust Me to know what's good for you, or will you choose for yourself?" The tree of the knowledge of good and evil stood in the garden as a choice and warning. Adam and Eve listened to the serpent and chose to trust their own knowledge, which was unreliable and influenced by pride, jealousy, anger, greed, and more. Now, with the arrival of sin, our own knowledge and motives are suspect and can distort our ability to discern what is and isn't from God.

My eight-year-old looks to me for advice as she navigates difficult relationships at school. I listen and give her wisdom that I have gained from my own heartache and hard-won experience. I know some of her choices will cause her heartache, but I can only offer her a better approach and encourage her to listen to my advice. When she does things her own way and winds up feeling hurt and disappointed, I comfort her and hope she'll trust that my way is better next time. I anticipate this cycle will be magnified as we enter the wilderness of puberty!

Despite Adam and Eve's choice, which ushered in the world's reality of sin and rebellion, God continues to have compassion on His people when they choose not to trust Him and rely on themselves instead. In response to the Israelites' bitterness and grumbling over the bitter water in the well, God provides a way for Moses to heal the water so they can drink it. Then, as He did in the garden, God offers them the opportunity to trust His wisdom and goodness more than their own pride and point of view.

Write It on Your Heart

Look up Exodus 15:26.

The Well of Our Hearts

In His Word, God points to His willingness to heal the water. But more than that, He heals people by removing whatever contaminates or corrupts them. God wants to heal the brokenness that distorts our view of Him and others.

Scripture paints the picture of our hearts being like a well. And just like the well at Marah, our hearts can also become bitter. People and circumstances will let us down. Despite our best efforts to remain upbeat, our hearts can become hardened from one too many disappointments.

Pray: Heavenly Father, we don't want bitterness to create barriers to loving You and others. We pray the blood of Jesus covers the bitterness and unforgiveness in our hearts. Remind us of the sweetness of Your love, which heals all wounds. In Jesus's name. Amen.

God doesn't want our hearts to become bitter because He knows it will hurt us and possibly the people around us. He offers the Israelites a way to live under His commands so they will be protected. Yet we see the Israelites and their descendants fail to trust and obey God.

Seven hundred years after the Israelites wandered in the wilderness, Hosea paints a difficult picture of Israel, declaring that her people would choose to "inquire of a piece of wood and their walking staff to give them oracles" rather than of the living God. Hosea captures God's ongoing struggle with His people, saying, they "have left their God to play a whore" (4:12).

Wow! That's a strong statement! What Hosea is getting at is that Israel, God's chosen nation, continues to give their lives and hearts to lowercase gods instead of Yahweh, who wants to be Israel's one true love.

We cannot remain in a perfect relationship with God, so God ultimately restores us through His Son's perfect obedience. God does what it takes to have a relationship with us in the middle of our mess and mess-ups, to heal the wounds that sin inflicts on us. Jesus calls Himself "the door of the sheep" (John 10:2). Ancient shepherds would stand at the narrow door of the pen, normally built as a low stone wall, and gently inspect each sheep for thorns, cuts, or other ailments that needed attention. God knows that our bitterness is a disease that will harm us. We don't just look at Jesus as a sacrifice for our salvation but as one who helps us heal from the wounds life inflicts.

In our Baptism, Jesus provided an entryway to God. God in human flesh bore "our sins in His body on the tree" (1 Peter 2:24) to exchange our sins and disobedience for His righteousness. Jesus' suffering and humility shame anyone who claims to be wise in his own eyes. God's upside-down kingdom is displayed as weakness becomes strength and Christ's wounds become our healing.

> [God] Himself bore our sins in His body on the tree, that we might die to sin and live to righteousness. By His wounds you have been healed. (1 Peter 2:24)

INVITATION

Do you identify with the idea that our hearts can become bitter like the well at Marah? *yes*

How can you look to God to protect your heart from bitterness? *Seek His forgiveness and then let it go... knowing God's in control.*

DAILY BREAD

Look up Hebrews 3:7–14. How did the Israelites harden their hearts to God's voice? How does the Holy Spirit keep our hearts tender toward God?

SAY GRACE

Enter His gates with thanksgiving,
and His courts with praise! Give
thanks to Him; bless His name!
(Psalm 100:4)

WEEK 4: DAY 5

Sympathizer

As I raise three children, I'm learning that I can parent with the short-term in mind or the long-term. There is always a fast fix that will quickly quiet my child's tantrums or complaints—but it isn't what will build our relationship and their character for the long term. If I'm committed to them for a lifetime, which I am, then I can choose the parenting tactic that might take more tears and more time but teaches them to be good humans.

God introduces a new name for Himself in Exodus 15. It shows that He is committed to His people for the long-term, not just the fast fix. God tells the Israelites that He is "the LORD, your healer," naming Himself "Yahweh-rapha" (Exodus 15:26). On the surface, we can think of this healing as a Band-Aid. Still, a deeper look at the Hebrew meaning shows that *rapha* also means to provide comfort, healing; or to provide care for, as in nursing someone to health and caring for them over time.

A common saying about effective leadership is "leaders climb the hill first." God doesn't take the quick-fix option for reconciliation or lead from the heavenly sidelines. He takes the long, tedious, and painful path of becoming human Himself to win our salvation. And when we look at how He lived His earthly life, we understand that He is showing us how to live. When we feel discouraged, we can remember God understands our human experiences and struggles and wants us to invite Him into them.

Let's look at a couple of Bible passages that paint this picture as we write down something about each that encourages us.

Philippians 2:7–9 *made Himself nothing, nature of a Servant, human likeness, humbled himself. Obedient to death — on a cross! He went through everything that I will ever experience*

Hebrews 4:15–16 *"we have one who has been tempted in every way, just as we are, but without sin.*

God invites His people to trust and obey Him. He also promises to heal them. Not waiting for the Israelites to prove their obedience, God keeps His end of the deal by offering them the rest and respite they need to recover from their difficult journey:

Then they came to Elim, where there were twelve springs of water and seventy palm trees, and they encamped there by the water. (Exodus 15:27)

Rapha also means "to be refreshed and repaired." God knew that the bitter well at Marah was just a brief march from the oasis of Elim, where the Israelites would get rest and restoration for their travel-weary bodies. We cannot know how God will provide when we are desperately thirsty or how He will turn bitter situations into sweet situations. We cannot yet see how the Marah valleys are just stopping points before we reach the goodness of Elim. But because He promises in His Word, we can trust that He is committed to our long-term health and not just the easy fix. Our Good Shepherd knows the whipping winds, the slippery mud, the steep climbs, and the bitterly cold nights. He commits to walking with us and softening the sting of the wilderness path.

Jesus identifies Himself as our Good Shepherd. It is through time and intimacy with their shepherd that sheep memorize his voice. Chambers describes faith as not just following an idea but a person:

Faith never knows where it is being led, but it loves and knows the One who is leading.[7]

Jesus did for us what God's Law could not do for the Israelites. The

Shepherd becomes the Lamb sacrificed, taking upon Himself the sin that divided us from God to heal our relationship with our Father and heal our hearts from guilt and shame. The Israelites go three days without water, and Jesus goes three days in the tomb. The bitter water at Marah is like the bitter water that spills from Jesus when His side is pierced, confirming He is dead. In Marah and at Golgatha, we see that God's healing is not an escape hatch from the struggles of this world. It is an invitation to freedom from struggle, persecution, thirst, and even death to life with Him.

> For I consider that the sufferings of this present time are not worth comparing with the glory that is to be revealed to us. For the creation waits with eager longing for the revealing of the sons of God. For the creation was subjected to futility, not willingly, but because of Him who subjected it, in hope that the creation itself will be set free from its bondage to corruption and obtain the freedom of the glory of the children of God. (Romans 8:18–21)

INVITATION

Are you in a season of Marah (bitterness), Elim (rest and resto-ration), or somewhere in between? *always both*

Have you thought of God as your Yahweh-rapha before? How can you invite Him into this role in your life?

DAILY BREAD

Look up Luke 10:25–37. Jesus is our Good Samaritan, our Jeho-vah-Rapha, who cares for us. What wounds do you need God to take care of?

SAY GRACE

Give us faith to trust You boldly,
Hope, to stay our souls on You;
But, oh, best of all Your graces,
With Your love our love renew. (*LSB* 851:4)

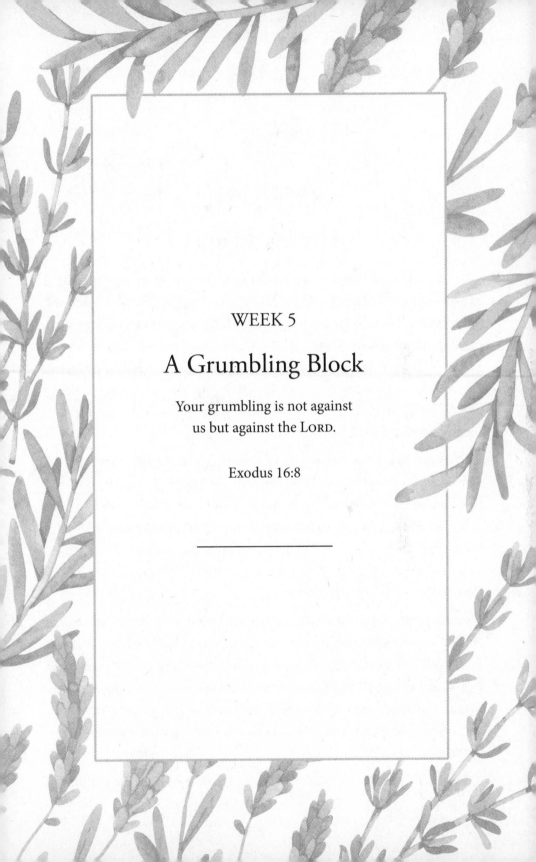

WEEK 5

A Grumbling Block

Your grumbling is not against
us but against the LORD.

Exodus 16:8

———————————

Hidden Manna

For the last five years, my husband and I have participated in a learning community that equips Christian men and women for leadership and discipleship. They have three-day gatherings for participants every six months, which means Nathan and I have to make space in our calendar to attend. Every time we've prepared to go, childcare has been complicated. But somehow, God has provided wonderful people to love our children like their own so we can participate in the gatherings where we grow spiritually and spend time together.

For the last gathering, we had the perfect plan in place. My parents arrived at our house to stay with the girls, including getting them to and from school. Since our two-year-old son, Boe, wasn't quite ready for an overnight away from us, we arranged for childcare in the area we would be staying. The day we were to leave, however, the person we'd arranged to watch Boe had to cancel. This meant that for the first time, my husband went to the gathering without me.

When I found out I'd have to stay home, I felt a rush of emotions: relief, frustration, jealousy, and maybe even a little anger. But as I had a moment to sit with this new reality, gratitude came whooshing in as I recognized that God had a different plan for me this time. Boe and I got to spend much-needed one-on-one time with my parents, who we don't get to see very often. God had provided for us in ways different from what He'd done in the past.

What if I hadn't seen God's generosity and kindness tucked within this small setback? Focusing so much on the past, I didn't recognize the new thing God was doing this time. As I asked these questions, I thought of where we are in our study of Exodus. Let's take a second look at chapter 16, when the Israelites faced a much more significant setback than mine: no food!

You would think they would have gotten the hang of this relying-on-God thing since, well . . . you know, the ten plagues, the Red Sea, and the bitter water made sweet. But following God is not a script we can follow or ten steps we complete perfectly. It is a relationship we cling to.

Yet again, as they face hunger, the Israelites grumble about their situation and remember the food they had as slaves in Egypt:

Would that we had died by the hand of the LORD in the land of Egypt, when we sat by the meat pots and ate bread to the full. (Exodus 16:3)

Of course, I know that my canceled childcare cannot compare with extreme hunger, but this was my small reminder to trust God as I learn to live in the present more and grumble less. Whether you are experiencing a setback big or small, you know the layered reality of your human fear and anxiety pressing against your desire to trust God. When our expectations don't line up with our realities, or worse, when we don't even recognize our reality because of hardship, we can get swept up in our sadness, regret, loneliness, disappointment, or fear that can lead us to grumble and long for the past.

This week, we will look at the cycle of grumbling, blaming, deflecting, and complaining that we can easily fall into when life gets uncomfortable and things don't go our way. And we will look at how we can cultivate a faith-filled response instead. We know that through Jesus, we have God's grace as we navigate the bumpy roads ahead with—ahem—not-so-graceful responses. Sometimes, when life isn't going my way, I can be a bad version of the seven dwarves: Grumpy, Mopey, Whiny, . . . well, you get the picture. But again and again, God invites us to look to Him.

Write It on Your Heart

Look up Matthew 11:29.

Today, I invite you to pay attention. Pay attention to frustrating interruptions and inconveniences. Like someone at work who is obstructing your progress, a friend who flaked, traffic, or a line at the grocery store. These could be more complicated, like caring for elderly parents, going to yet another doctor appointment, or meeting with the principal at your child's school. What is God inviting you to do with this setback?

Maybe God is asking you to trust in His timing, exhale a prayer instead of an angry retort, or rely on Him for strength to do hard things. What does it look like to have a more open posture to where God is inviting you to lean in? Our lives are full of inconveniences and disrupted plans—some small and some that rearrange the landscape of our lives. Both are an invitation to receive God's manna today.

During the first week of our study, we looked at how God's provision and blessing can come with struggle, uncertainty, and even setbacks. We paused to recognize what this looked like in our present realities. I encourage you to continue to make room for this practice in your life as we pray that God would give us eyes of faith to see His blessings in hard things and soften our hearts. As we practice finding God's manna in our wilderness struggles, we train our hearts to respond differently to disappointment and loss. We know, however, that we can't do this by our own effort. The Holy Spirit is with us, comforting us and working with us as we pray and process our difficult realities.

As you face doubt and heartache in an unfamiliar landscape of struggle and uncertainty, I pray that you learn to scan the horizon for God's manna, which comes each morning. We can work on seeing, with gratitude, how God has guided us in the past and look with anticipation to how He will meet our needs today.

INVITATION

Do you ever find yourself longing for past circumstances? Explain.

If so, how might you redirect your focus to what God is doing in your life today?

DAILY BREAD

Look up Matthew 6:31–33. How has God been your provider? How can you remember His provision to give you courage in your moments of need? *" what shall we eat or what shall we drink — your heavenly father knows that you need them — Seek first His kingdom + righteousness + all these things will be given to you as well. Priorities -> God will provide*

SAY GRACE

Blessed is the man who trusts in the LORD, whose trust is the LORD. He is like a tree planted by water, that sends out its roots by the stream, and does not fear when heat comes, for its leaves remain green, and is not anxious in the year of drought, for it does not cease to bear fruit. (Jeremiah 17:7–8)

God-Formed Perspective

Is it just me, or have you ever regarded grumbling as somewhat harmless? For too long, I didn't take grumbling seriously. But the more I study the Book of Exodus, the more I recognize that grumbling is a symptom of rebellious hearts that doubt and deny God.

Anyone who has spent time with an eight-year-old on a road trip knows that grumbling is a symptom of the sinful human condition. Because of sin, our human hearts do not always trust God's goodness, making it easy for us to give in to fear, doubt, jealousy, and anger—all selfish emotions that are the seedbed for grumbling. But perhaps it is possible to sidestep grumbling and respond in faith instead when these emotions are stirred in our hearts. Yes, even if we have done our share of grumbling in the past (I know I have!), I believe another option is waiting for us.

As we revisited the Israelites in the wilderness of sin on day one this week, we saw that they were so focused on their circumstances that they had lost touch with reality. Not only were they idealizing their past as slaves in Egypt, but they questioned Moses and Aaron's intentions, ultimately questioning God's character. We looked at this passage before, but let's look at verse 3 again for context:

> Would that we had died by the hand of the Lord in the land of Egypt, when we sat by the meat pots and ate bread to the full, for you [Moses] have brought us out into this wilderness to kill this whole assembly with hunger. (Exodus 16:3)

Are they talking about the same Egypt we read about in the first chapter of Exodus, where it says, "They ruthlessly made the people of Israel work as slaves" (1:13)? God used Moses to save the Israelites from harsh labor and poor living conditions. But they are thinking only of their biggest problem at that moment. The vicious thing gnawing at them: hunger. The low rumble of discontent grows to a deafening roar as they hurl anger, resentment, and disbelief at Moses and Aaron—the easy targets standing right in front of them.

Sin entered the world the same way when Satan sucked Eve into his right-now reality and her human desire. Had Eve hit pause, taken a deep breath, and thought about her options, had she remembered God's words for guidance, she might not have given into the tyranny of "right now." But any salesman will tell you that the minute someone walks away from the negotiation to "think things over," the sale is lost.

One verse I often employ when I'm tempted to give into the urgency of negative emotions or an immediate craving is, "Resist the devil, and he will flee from you" (James 4:7). That snake slithers back into the hole he came from.

Moses knows not to get sucked into this illusion. In this escalating crisis, where the people demand bread "right now," even in a state of fear and uncertainty, Moses turns to God. The death drum beats loudly as the people grow faint. Hunger growls and threatens to shred their last threads of humanity. Their food sacks are bare, and so is the desert. But Moses looks to God. In the face of scarcity, amid the roar of hundreds of thousands of grumbling people, he knows God's resources are unlimited.

Satan wants us to look at our right-now needs and urges us to focus on what's right in front of our noses. Rather than getting sucked into the evil one's limited perspective, God shapes Moses' perspective so he recognizes another reality. Moses sees the problem isn't food; it is trust. As Moses and Aaron share God's plan to provide meat and bread with the people, Moses presses them, "What are we? Your grumbling is not against us but against the Lord" (Exodus 16:8).

Pray: God, we know that You want to fulfill more than our right-now needs. But we recognize that we often struggle to look beyond the problem or need right in front of us. Lord, we pray that we would elevate our gaze from the present moment so that we might fix our eyes on Jesus, our conqueror. Help us trust You more fully so we can rest in Your provision today and Your wisdom for our future. In Jesus' name. Amen.

Spiritual Food

Jesus teaches us about food and water that isn't the kind we consume to fill our bellies, but that satisfies us nonetheless. In John 4, Jesus had just taught the Samaritan woman at the well about the living water—that is, the Holy Spirit—and testified to her that He is the Messiah. Then, when the disciples arrive and urge Jesus to eat, He continues His lesson, saying, "I have food to eat that you do not know about" (John 4:32). Jesus had just taught the Samaritan woman about the water that comes from the Holy Spirit, but what is this food He speaks of? Jesus explains, "My food is to do the will of Him who sent Me and to accomplish His work" (John 4:34).

We also see the relationship between water and bread in the accounts of Jesus' Baptism and temptation in the wilderness. Jesus is baptized in the Jordan River, and the Holy Spirit descends upon Him in the form of a dove. After Jesus receives spiritual water in Baptism, the Father sends Him into the wilderness to fast for forty days. There He is tempted by Satan. When Satan tempts Jesus to turn stones into bread, notice how Jesus responds.

Write It on Your Heart

Look up Matthew 4:4. *Jesus answered, "It is written . . . Man does not live on bread alone, but on every word that comes from the mouth of God"*

Jesus points to a food that is not physical but spiritual. He wants us to hunger and thirst for more than food and water, which only temporarily meet our needs.

In the same way, God provides for the Israelites' physical needs, but He wants them to crave and seek something greater. He wants them to crave a relationship with Him and seek His will, which would bring them ultimate fulfillment. Instead, the Israelites look away from God and focus on their hunger. They doubt and grumble against God. Moses has journeyed with God since the burning bush and learned to put trust in Him alone, not in his circumstances. Because Moses has a deep relationship with God, he focuses more on who God is than on what is happening around him.

We can find hope in Moses' example as we look to God to provide spiritual food that gives us faith as we face unmet needs. The waters of Baptism assure us of God's promises as the Holy Spirit gives us the faith we need to keep going. God's Word gives us the truth that directs our gaze toward Jesus. We take Jesus' body and blood in the bread and wine of the Holy Supper and remember that Jesus died and rose again so that we can be sustained into eternal life with Him.

How has God shown His faithfulness in your life? Gratitude recognizes God's ongoing presence in our lives. It reveals His heart for us. It's not about what we can do for God or what we can get from Him. Our God wants nothing more than to establish trust in our hearts through His Word and Sacraments, through which He empowers us to do His will. As a Father who cares for His children, He doesn't just want to provide for our right-now needs but also our long-term spiritual needs, such as a church home and opportunities to serve others.

INVITATION

Do you ever feel tempted to focus on your right-now needs and lose sight of God?

After reading this chapter, how will you respond the next time a right-now need arises? Do you need something right now?

Look up Matthew 4:1–4. How can we live by "every word that comes from the mouth of God" today? *put God & His word first - daily, to give us focus for the day.*

SAY GRACE

Therefore, as you received Christ Jesus the Lord,
so walk in Him, rooted and built up
in Him and established in the faith,
just as you were taught, abounding in thanksgiving.
(Colossians 2:6–7)

WEEK 5: DAY 3

Broken Mirrors

A pair of women who came to my family's church were named Moan and Groan. Okay, so those were nicknames I was told. I can't remember their actual names. And I write this with regret because I realize their nicknames are not kind. But these ladies seemed impossible to get to know, despite my best efforts to break the ice. They'd show up every few months, keeping their distance with puckered looks on their faces. Before the services even ended, they'd exit to the parking lot. A couple of days later, the church would receive a letter with a laundry list of all the ways we were doing things wrong. To some, perhaps, these women were known as loving mothers, sisters, and friends. To others, they had names. But in my brief encounters with them, their identities were swallowed up by their discontentment.

How can our discontentment and grumbling distort our identity as God's children? Many cathedrals are famous for elaborate ceilings. Some cathedrals provide large hand mirrors so that you can comfortably take in the beautiful view by looking down at the reflection instead of up at the ceiling. But if someone commented on how beautiful the mirror was, they would be missing the point. The mirror is only a tool to view the true beauty of the cathedral ceiling. And if that mirror became cracked, it would no longer be able to fully reflect the gilded beauty above.

God created us in His image to reflect Him. When we become bitter, discontent, and resentful, however, and respond with complaining, arguing, and grumbling, we create disunity instead of unity and strife instead of peace. That is why it is so important to God that we look to Him to renew our minds.

Write It on Your Heart

Look up Romans 12:2. Do not conform any longer to the pattern of this world but be transformed by the renewing of your mind. Then you will be able to test and approve what God's will is - His good, perfect, + pleasing will.

In Paul's Letter to the Philippians, he encouraged them to "do all things without grumbling or disputing" (Philippians 2:14). He had two distinct purposes in mind:

- to maintain peace and unity among the people

- to keep ourselves blameless and innocent

Paul goes on to explain that we should remain blameless so that we might "shine as lights in the world" (2:15). If you're like me, the song "This Little Light of Mine" just popped into your head. The theology you might have heard as a child points to why our grumbling can be so harmful. God created us to shine His light and strive to live pure and blameless lives. Of course, what ultimately makes us blameless before God is Jesus' sacrifice on our behalf. But as believers, we are encouraged and empowered to live differently because of who God calls us to be as His children.

This doesn't mean we won't be tempted to give into bitterness, grumbling, or arguing in the face of difficult people and circumstances. The wilderness can leave us hungry, tired, angry, grieving, or disappointed—sometimes all at the same time, which can be a recipe for our worst selves to come out. Sometimes, my worst self comes out before my first cup of coffee in the morning! Despite these setbacks, we are invited into a vision that is bigger than us. As we pursue a God-shaped perspective and God-shaped identity, we are children who reflect God to people who desperately need a glimpse of Him.

God was among the Israelites, bringing about astounding miracles, but we experience God's miracle every day.

Before Paul exhorts the Philippians not to grumble, he reminds them that because of the Holy Spirit,

It is _____God_____ who works in _____you_____, both to _____will_____ and to _____act according_____ for His good pleasure. (Philippians 2:13)
(purpose)

God empowers us to respond by faith as we participate in the Spirit's will for us to live in peace and unity instead of in bitterness and division. Our new identity is not defined by the disappointments of this world but by the promises of Jesus. *faith + obedience can not be separated*

INVITATION

Has discontentment ever distorted your view of God and others?

yes

How can you look to God to renew your mind today?

Be in the Word & pray with that intention in mind

DAILY BREAD

Look up Philippians 2:12–17. What is the "word of life" that Paul encourages believers to hold fast to?

SAY GRACE

God came to us then at Pentecost,
His Spirit new life revealing,
That we might no more from Him be lost,
All darkness for us dispelling.
His flame will the mark of sin efface
And bring to us all His healing. (*LSB* 503:4)

WEEK 5: DAY 4

Grumbling or Lamenting?

The last two times I moved, I was also pregnant. Raging hormones gave my emotions sharp edges, and my urge to nest made me feel restless. Moving is arduous, so if I didn't take time to be with God in prayer or process what I was going through in a meaningful conversation with a friend, my anxieties would come out as meltdowns. With my life in transition and my home in boxes, I often became ill-tempered and argumentative to relieve the tension and uncertainty.

This might also describe the Israelites' behavior. God wants to use their time in the wilderness to train their hearts to trust Him. But instead, they drift further from Him as they quarrel, grumble, and blame.

The Bible shows two different types of complaining: one that is acceptable to God and one that is not. Let's take a look at each:

Faithless grumbling is defined as "to complain about someone or something in an annoyed way."

Faith-filled lamenting is defined as "to express sadness" and "to feel sorry about something."

While faithless grumbling is complaining about God, a faith-filled lament expresses anguish toward God. Faithless grumbling shows a lack of faith by complaining as though God can't hear us—as though He is impotent to help or change what is happening. In contrast, faithful lamenting shows faith and persistence as we press into God, even when we don't understand or see how God can help us. Grumbling takes a posture of pride. Lamenting takes a posture of humility and trust.

A lament, which we find throughout Scripture, is a fervent expression of one's grief or sadness. David is the author of many laments in the Book of Psalms. Some might say he had a flare for the dramatic: "I am weary with my moaning; every night I flood my bed with tears" (Psalm 6:6). But David was the one the prophet Samuel said was a man after God's own heart (see 1 Samuel 13:14). David was hunted by King Saul, bedded another man's wife, and then had her husband murdered. He lost one of his sons and was painfully betrayed by another. All the while, rather than grumbling about God, David cried out to Him

- in repentance: "Create in me a clean heart, O God" (Psalm 51:10);

- in trust: "You are my rock and my fortress" (Psalm 31:3); and

- in love and loyalty: "He has wondrously shown His steadfast love to me" (Psalm 31:21).

David recognized God was the only one able to bring him justice and peace.

Like the Israelites, David was also familiar with the wilderness. He grew up in the wilderness as a shepherd and hid in the wilderness while being hunted by Saul. David wasn't just passing the time in the wilderness. He was drawing closer to God. The Bible shows the wilderness as a place of transformation and encounter with God for many of His people. God spoke to Abraham, Moses, and Elijah in the wilderness. John the Baptist is introduced in the Bible as "the voice of one crying in the wilderness" (Matthew 3:3).

With this context, we see that God isn't just leading the Israelites through the wilderness but to the wilderness. It's part of His itinerary. In the wilderness, God wants to meet, guide, and teach the Israelites. He wants them to talk with Him in prayer as He speaks to them through Moses.

Pray: Father, we pray that You would meet us in the places where we feel like we are in a wilderness. We know we are never hidden from You. We pray that You would meet us, teach us, and remind us of who we are in Jesus. In Jesus' name. Amen.

God's Wilderness Whispers

The Hebrew word for *wilderness* is pronounced "midbar," but because there are no vowels in the Hebrew language, it is spelled *mdbr*. In addition, the Hebrew word pronounced "medaber," from the verb "to speak," is spelled the same way (*mdbr*). God brought the Israelites into the wilderness (*midbar*), so He could speak (*medaber*) to them. Their response to this invitation can be to turn toward Him in relationship, as He helps them through their feelings of fear and desperation, or to become isolated and resentful toward God and one another.

There is much to learn from the Israelites' experience. Do you feel like you are in a wilderness? Is your resentment growing as your circumstances seem stagnant? The word *liminal* describes the state of being on a threshold to something. Liminal means the place where we've left one thing behind but are waiting to arrive at the next destination.

Like my experience with moving while pregnant, there are many seasons in life when we can experience liminality. For many women, pregnancy or the adoption process is a liminal experience. Their hearts know they are the mother of a child, but they can't yet hold him in their arms. A move is also a liminal experience as your old home becomes a temporary space while you wait to transition to your new home. My sister experienced a year of liminality when she was battling breast cancer. Chemotherapy and other treatments caused crippling sickness and side effects that prevented her from living her normal life, but she knew the treatments would end and her regular activities would resume.

We choose some liminal experiences, and some are thrust upon us. When we enter a liminal space in wilderness moments, we are invited to reconsider who we are and who God is. Sidelined, we have time to think more deeply about our identity and purpose. These seasons become a test of whether we, too, will grumble in doubt or, in faith, lament to our Creator. But even when we grumble, we can trust that God is with us, speaking through His Spirit and using the season (that could be considered a waste) as a womb, where He gently reforms us into who He calls us to be. While the Israelites see the wilderness as a place to be loathed, from our vantage point, we can see the wilderness as the birthplace of renewed faith and deeper dependence on God.

INVITATION

In your wilderness seasons, do you feel closer to God or further away?

How can God speak (medaber) to you in the season you are in right now?

DAILY BREAD

Look up Psalm 63:1–8. This psalm was written by David when he was hiding in the wilderness from King Saul. How did David respond to his physical need and distress? How does this encourage you? *trusts & glorifies God - praise*

SAY GRACE

The Lord is my strength and my shield;
in Him my heart trusts, and I am helped;
my heart exults, and with my song
I give thanks to Him. (Psalm 28:7)

WEEK 5: DAY 5

Rest from Grumbling

How do you spend your days off? Many see a day off work as a chance to run errands, meal prep, and do laundry. God gives the Israelites a day off for the sole purpose of rest. This is meaningful because although the Israelites have been dreaming of full bellies in Egypt, their reality as slaves was food rations, harsh work conditions, and few (if any) days off. God first demonstrated Sabbath rest in Genesis when He rested from creating the universe after six days (see Genesis 2:3). God didn't need physical rest. We have learned that He is omnipotent, meaning His power never diminishes. But in Genesis 2, He paused to enjoy what He had created. God designed Sabbath for the Israelites to point them to a greater rest that wouldn't be fulfilled for nearly 1,500 years.

After the people grumble for food, God tells Moses He will "rain bread from heaven," but it will come with a test (Exodus 16:4). The Israelites are to collect what they need each day and not store any extra. When some people try to save the bread for another day, "it bred worms and stank" (16:20).

On the sixth day, God provides twice as much bread so they can take "a day of solemn rest, a holy Sabbath to the Lord" (16:23). It isn't surprising that some of the people still go outside to look for manna, only to find the landscape bare. They quickly learn that God doesn't want them to rely on their resourcefulness but to look to Him alone for the daily bread they need. God alone provides manna that comes with the dew while they sleep and just enough food to rest from their work on the Sabbath.

God is teaching them a greater lesson than just their reliance on Him for food. Their day of rest isn't filled with distractions like Nintendo, *Downton Abbey*, or a good book. It isn't even filled with the distraction of taking time to prepare food. As they rest in their tents, God is physically reminding them that their status as God's chosen nation is not a status they have done anything to earn; it is a gift of His grace. On Mount Sinai, God said that His Sabbaths are a sign for the Israelites and future generations to remember that "I, the LORD, sanctify you" (Exodus 31:13).

However, this doesn't stop God's people from trying to earn brownie points. Before Jesus arrives on the scene, the Pharisees had turned the Sabbath into the spiritual Olympics to earn religious gold metals. They create thirty-nine categories for work-related activities, stipulating rules to maintain control and the moral high ground. The problem is that God intended to remind His people that He alone made them holy.

Jesus says, "The Sabbath was made for man, not man for the Sabbath," reminding us that God's intentions are not to burden His people with more religious hoops to jump through but that He is our provider (Mark 2:27).

The Lord God is your provider. Do you need to rest in that knowledge right now? You do not keep the world spinning despite how much your head is spinning with all you need to get done today. How are you taking time to pause and rest in God?

Here is another reality worth considering. Work was made for man, not man for work. When we make our productivity the same badge of honor as the Pharisees tried to earn with their Olympic rest, it becomes the same obstacle of personal achievement that stands between us and the relationship God desires to have with us.

Opening the Gift

How often do we grumble about all our work and to-dos, as though our doing is what keeps our world in order? We also need to be reminded of the Sabbath gift that refocuses our hearts on God, who makes us holy. Although God offers the Israelites a Sabbath rest, they still rely on the Law to remain in right relationship with God. The Law God gives Moses and the sacrifices the Israelites make were intended to point them to the forgiveness He will provide in the fulfillment of that Law, Christ Jesus. But the Israelites' grumbling and self-focus draw their attention from God to their own needs and desires.

To bring the rest that God truly desires for us, He came as a man to fulfill the Law and be the final sacrifice for sin. In this way, Jesus is our Sabbath, and God's new covenant becomes rest, not just for the Israelites, but for all nations. Jesus removes the burdensome Law that stands between us and God through His atoning blood. He brings us into God's presence for ultimate rest in Him. Jesus is our Sabbath rest.

Write It on Your Heart

Look up Hebrews 4:9–10. *There remains then a Sabbath-rest for the people of God. For anyone who enters God's rest also rests from his own work, just as God did from His.*

INVITATION

Do you take a day or scheduled hours to rest from work and obligations?

How might Sabbath rest help you grumble less and appreciate God more?

DAILY BREAD

Look up Exodus 16:25–27. How are these verses speaking to you today? What words or phrases stand out? Why?

SAY GRACE

You keep him in perfect peace whose mind is
stayed on You, because he trusts in You. (Isaiah 26:3)

WEEK 6

Hidden Manna

The water that I will give him will
become in him a spring of water
welling up to eternal life.

John 4:14

———

To Whom Shall We Go?

I despise water fountains. I know my sentiment sounds strong, but let me explain. Unlike my children, I didn't grow up bringing a fancy insulated and personalized water bottle to school. None of the kids did. We didn't even bring plain plastic water bottles to school. All thirty of the hot, sweaty, and thirsty kids in my class relied on the one tiny stream of water from the fountain in front of our classroom to rehydrate after returning from outdoor recess in the hot sun. (Shade structures weren't much of a thing in those days either.) We lined up, single file, and as each of us drank, the others would count to ten. Desperately thirsty kids would try to squeeze in one or two more seconds, but the children behind them were adamant. "You're done!" they'd chant as they began kicking the child's heels or calling for a teacher. Just thinking about it today makes me thirsty and a bit traumatized.

You might share similar experiences of unquenched thirst. You know water is the one pressing need in this desperate state—an aching thought that consumes your very being. As we enter our sixth week of study together, we encounter the thirsty Israelites, who are desperate and downright hostile toward Moses because he can't supply the one thing their bodies are shouting for. We read in Exodus 17 that the people had left the wilderness of Sin in stages to camp at Rephidim, "but there was no water for the people to drink" (Exodus 17:1). No water! Not even a ten-second sip to ease the burn in their throats.

Have you ever been in a desperate situation where you had an urgent need? Have you prayed that God would ease your pain and give you peace as you went through crippling anxiety? a difficult childbirth? chemotherapy? chronic pain? Have you gone through emotional pain? a divorce? betrayal? loss of a loved one? You plead, pray, beg, and ball your fists, but a solution is like sand slipping through your tight grip. No person can help. There's no way around, no shortcut, and no way over. There's not even a trapdoor for escape. The only way is through. Through the desperation, through the hurt, through the rocky terrain on your blistered, achy feet. You are forced to push through the long, cold nights when you sit in your suffering, the wind whipping at your wounds and howling hopelessness.

Some might call this a "dark night of the soul," and I imagine you can remember a time when you or someone you love has suffered through this kind of a hopeless season. With your needs beyond your fingertips, did you experience dismay and desperation during this season? Anger? Then you can empathize with the emotional state of the hostile Israelites who are consumed by their need.

The place they camp, Rephidim, is a Hebrew word that possibly means "place of rest." If this sounds incongruent, then you are on to something. Oddly enough, the camp where God leads them to "rest" has no water. Yes, the Israelites have followed the pillar of cloud and fire to the place He instructed; and God has led them to a place where there is no water. They are in the will of God, but they are not experiencing the provision of God. How can this be?

I want to let you in on a little promise—five words with big importance—as we navigate deserts and dark nights:

Where God leads, God provides.

Let's pause and write those words below to help them sink in.

Where God ___*leads*___, God ___*provides*___.

Isaiah talks about a future for God's people that is available for us through Jesus.

Write It on Your Heart

Look up Isaiah 58:11. *The Lord will guide you always; He will satisfy your needs in an unscorched land and will strengthen your frame. You will be like a well-watered garden, like a spring whose waters never fail.*

God knows His people need to be sustained not just physically but also spiritually as they turn to Him. If they ask, He will provide. Yet they are still spiritually blind to the unlimited provision God wants to supply as they abide in relationship with Him. Sometimes, it is only when we face the scarcity of this world that we thirst and hunger for God. Through Jesus, God sends His Spirit to make us watered gardens that grow fruit, not just in spite of but through our suffering and hardship. God does not create suffering, but He may let us walk through it to experience our need for Him. And in this desperate place, He provides.

> And my God will supply every need of yours according to His riches in glory in Christ Jesus. (Philippians 4:19)

The Israelites don't see their physical needs as a symptom of their greater need for their Provider and Sustainer. As the one who sustains, God becomes our life source, not just our meal source.

Let's look at the definition of the words *provide* and *sustain* to see the difference.

1. Provide: "to supply or make available (something wanted or needed)."[8]

2. Sustain: "to give support or relief to"; "to supply"; "to nourish"; "to support the weight of."[9]

God not only (1.) *provides for our needs*, He (2.) *sustains, supports, & nourishes us.*

As sustainer, God is the one who gives the Israelites breath and life and all they need to flourish—even in a barren land. God doesn't just give us what we need, He gives us Himself.

INVITATION

Have you been through "a dark night of the soul"? Describe it
here. If you haven't, describe a difficult situation someone you
love has endured. *death of a child, cancer, dementia*

How has this experience invited you to rely on God more?
In these situations there is nothing we can do but depend on God's provision & strength.

DAILY BREAD

Read Exodus 17:1–7. What is Moses' response to the Israelites?
How does God respond? (Note how their responses contrast.)
Asks God what should I do with these people – these complainers. God tells Moses to take some elders & go to the rock at Horeb & hit the rock with his staff & got water

SAY GRACE

The steadfast love of the Lord never ceases;

His mercies never come to an end; they

are new every morning; great is Your faithfulness.

(Lamentations 3:22–23)

WEEK 6: DAY 2

Words of Eternal Life

The man was paralyzed. He could no longer speak, let alone walk. But as he took his last breaths, his family waved good-bye as though he were merely leaving the room. One day, he was their rock. The next, he became like an immovable stone, sunk into a hospital bed. They watched his life slowly leak out of him. Yet their faith gave them enough courage to trust that they saw only part of the reality. At his death, they whispered, "Thank You, God," as their hearts found rest in an unseen future where their dad's broken body would be restored and perfected so that he could walk, dance, and hug them one day in an eternal promised land.

Some might shake their heads at this family with unshakeable faith in the face of life's worst outcome. They might say whoever believes there is life after death and a God who cares about our eternity is out of their minds. They would be right. This family is out of their sinful human minds because the only way to believe spiritual truths is with the mind of Christ. The mind of Christ is given to us by the Spirit of God, as we see God's hidden wisdom, which is now revealed to us in Jesus. To those without God's Spirit, these things are foolish; but we know that God's wisdom is in sharp contrast to man's wisdom.

Write It on Your Heart

Look up 1 Corinthians 1:18. *For the message of the cross is foolishness to those who are perishing but to us who are being saved it is the power of God*

As we reposition ourselves in the exodus narrative, we enter a moment tense with disappointment and desperation. The Israelites are out of water and full of bitterness. In that moment of life-threatening need, they focus their eyes on the waterless wasteland and harden their hearts to God's reality. We see this pattern depicted in Scripture throughout the nation's history. The people witness God's wonders, yet many do not turn to Him for guidance and understanding. This is a pattern we, too, can fall into if we look only at our problems and present realities and forget God's presence.

God doesn't promise to answer every prayer in the ways we expect, but He does promise to hear every prayer and respond according to His will for us. In our present circumstances, Paul tells us that "all things work together for good, for those who are called according to His purpose" (Romans 8:28). He keeps His promise to provide us with forgiveness and a future in eternity with Him. Therefore, we can cling to God's promise that His full peace and restoration will happen in the life to come. This means trusting that God is good here and now, even if His provision isn't something we can make sense of now.

The reality of God's provision today is visible in the Church as we see imperfect people sanctified to be Jesus' hands and feet. We touch and taste the reality of God's forgiveness and Jesus' sacrificial love in the Holy Supper, where He gives His very body and blood, which He gave for us on the cross. His grace touches us in Baptism as water makes us holy through God's presence and promise. We chew on the reality of God's truth in His Word, which strengthens and renews our faith.

God's provision comes to us in peace and joy in impossible circumstances, impossible prayers answered, and in God's Spirit, which prompts us to choose to love and forgive others when our own hearts bend toward bitterness. But even as we experience God in these real ways when the world wears on us, it can feel like our faith also wears thin. Then we are tempted to question if He is real and working in our lives.

Asking the Hard Question

"Is the LORD among us or not?" (Exodus 17:7). The Israelites ask that question with incredulity as they reach their camp and can't find drinkable water. During their journey, they had witnessed a spectacular show of God's supernatural power. Still, it appears that the wonder of God's miracles have worn into an ordinary experience amid the stress of their everyday struggle. Perhaps when you see bread from heaven on the ground before you every day, such provision becomes something you expect rather than an astounding gift.

The wilderness challenges us to realize that God doesn't belong in the religious trappings of faith on our terms but in the wild and untrod territory of unmet wants intermingling with miracles and wonder that brings us to our knees. God uses the wilderness to get His truth from our heads into our hearts—like the manna that satisfies physical hunger and nourishes faith.

It's like going to an amazing Christian retreat and feeling inspired to change the world, only to return to a regular Monday and forget everything except our desperate need for coffee. In the wilderness, no longer insulated from the harsh realities of a broken world that cannot satisfy, God shows us our need for Him. As we see ourselves in the Israelites' journey, we can consider how their question can be one we whisper when our faith feels worn from wandering and waiting on God: "Is the LORD among us or not?" As we ask and wait, He cultivates our character and fortifies our faith.

Sometimes it is hard to reconcile our difficult realities with the knowledge that God is present and working in our lives. The Israelites have been wandering. They are weary, tired of traveling, worn out, and in need of water. If God is with them, why are they in that desperate place? But they aren't alone in questioning God. It seems that questioning God is wired into our sinful nature. John the Baptist was sent by God to prepare the way for the coming Messiah. But once Jesus arrives, John finds himself sitting in jail awaiting execution. He sends his disciples to ask Jesus, "Are You the one who is to come, or shall we look for another?" (Matthew 11:3).

We question God, and He gives us answers we don't expect. Our human nature wants God to operate on our terms and in our timing, but God shifts our human understanding into His upside-down kingdom. Jesus doesn't bring God's kingdom in the way the Jews expect, just as the Israelites think God isn't providing for them.

Jesus said of John the Baptist, "Among those born of women none is greater than John" (Luke 17:28). Yet at the end of his short ministry, John sat immobilized in a jail cell.

If God fails to meet our standards and expectations, it's easy for our human minds to ask, "Are You really here, God? Do You really know what You're doing, God?" Our questions tumble from us as we overlook His answers before us. When we are so busy straining our eyes for what we're hoping God will do, we can miss what He is already doing.

The Pharisees ask when the kingdom of God will come. Jesus gives an answer they cannot grasp.

Look up Luke 17:21 and complete the sentence: _The kingdom of God is within you._

The kingdom of God _is_ _in_ _the_ _midst_ _of_ _you_.

It is by God's Spirit that we receive faith that sustains us, even when we feel weary and doubtful. God provides for us through His Word and Sacraments just as surely as He provides manna and water for the doubting Israelites. Although this generation of Israelites never grasps the things of God, as believers today, we know the mysteries hidden for us in Christ Jesus. Our crucified Jesus, who was laid dead behind the stone, didn't remain there; three days later, He walked out of the tomb.

INVITATION

Where is God inviting you to walk by faith in the face of doubt today?

DAILY BREAD

Look up Matthew 11:1–15. What stands out to you about Jesus' response to the question John's disciples asked Him?

Does this challenge you to look at present circumstances in a new way?

SAY GRACE

So they took away the stone. And Jesus
lifted up His eyes and said, "Father, I thank
You that You have heard Me." (John 11:41)

Deep Roots, Delicious Fruit

Instead of a green thumb, I have a brown thumb. Most plants under my care wind up brown and bone dry. The only plants I manage to keep alive are drought-tolerant ones that can adapt to my erratic or nonexistent watering schedule. When we lived in Arizona, my brown thumb thrived! I was able to keep a whole plot of plants alive. I quickly gained an appreciation for drought-tolerant landscapes because where we lived, a grass lawn that required constant watering was considered extravagant. My desert-scape yard was covered in crushed granite and dotted with the soft colors and smells of English lavender, spicebush, and rosemary.

As I've spent time exploring the concept of the wilderness and the conditions the Israelites survived in, my curiosity led me to investigate the unique characteristics of drought-tolerant plants and what enables them to thrive in hot and dry conditions. I discovered that to survive, they must grow an extensive root system that has greater breadth and depth than plants that grow in wetter climates.

With all this talk about plants, it is worth looking at how often the Bible talks about plants, from the tree of life and the infamous fruit to bitter herbs, cedars of Lebanon, olive trees, and grapevines. With a bit of digging (see what I did there?), I'm beginning to understand that through nature and plants, God is teaching us much deeper spiritual truths that we can continue to unearth and apply to our lives today. (I couldn't resist that last one.)

One illustration that especially resonates is how the Bible compares us to a tree that grows roots and bears fruit. If we are like trees that grow roots, do we want our roots to have the breadth and depth that help us endure harsh, hot weather? How do we produce fruit? And how do we ensure our fruit is the good kind and not something like a bad apple?

These are all worthy questions that I want to look at in the context of our Bible account. Jesus tells us that seeds planted in good soil receive God's Word, which gives them "an honest and good heart, and bear fruit and patience" (Luke 8:15).

This generation of Israelites hear from God and experience God, but in the face of adverse conditions in the wilderness, they don't demonstrate how they should cling to God and persevere. Instead, the fruit they produce is quarreling with Moses and testing the Lord. However, faithful Moses demonstrates what deep spiritual roots looks like as he pushes past the uncertainty and testing and looks to God for the sustenance the Israelites need. We can look to another Old Testament leader, King David, as a model of what it looks like to grow roots into God in the face of adversity.

The Fruit in Us

As we read earlier, King David faced suffering and uncertainty. As a result, he sinks his roots into the heart of God (see 1 Samuel 13:14). In his want and need, rather than just craving earthly comforts, David thirsts for God:

> O God, You are my God; earnestly I seek You; my soul thirsts for You; my flesh faints for You, as in a dry and weary land where there is no water. So I have looked upon You in the sanctuary, beholding Your power and glory. Because Your steadfast love is better than life, my lips will praise You. So I will bless You as long as I live; in Your name I will lift up my hands. (Psalm 63:1–4)

As David reaches out to God to satisfy his spiritual thirst in a place of desperate need, God produces fruit in him. God uses David for many great things, but the humble fruit God generates does not spring from David's strength, handsome looks, cunning, or even his song of faith; it is from

God's response to his noble and good heart. David has a heart that produces fruit "in keeping with repentance" (Matthew 3:8) and "the fruit of lips that acknowledge His name" (Hebrews 13:15).

How can we live lives that also flow from a noble and good heart like David? The author of Hebrews talks about the "people of old" who held fast to their faith in the face of difficult circumstances. Following these verses, in Chapter 13, the author talks about a practical way we exercise our faith and, in doing so, bear good fruit. Let's look at the verse together.

Write It on Your Heart

Look up Hebrews 13:15.

David demonstrates a life punctuated by worship and trust in the face of struggle and uncertainty. We can read and treasure it throughout the psalms. His worship isn't the sort that was written from a life of ease but in the struggle of human emotions and difficult circumstances. In the same way, the writer of Hebrews doesn't imply that the fruit of praise is something that bursts from us with ease. The hallelujah that is cried in hardship is like the prayer of King Jehosophat in the face of a massive approaching army.

Look up 2 Chronicles 20:12.

Do you need to speak this verse over your difficult circumstances today? "I don't know what to do about losing my job, God, but I will look to You to provide." "I don't know whether this biopsy will be malignant, God, but even if it is, I will look to You for help and healing." "I don't know how I will get through this day, God; the grief feels so heavy, but I will look to You for the strength I need."

It is in the seasons of fear and desperation or even apathy when faith feels like picking rocks, or when the thorns and weeds threaten to choke out our hope that we have the opportunity to offer "a sacrifice of praise" that results in spiritual fruit.

We can fall into the trap of seeing this time in the Israelites' journey as a test they either pass or fail. But then we would miss the beautiful glimpse of God's character. God is committed to guiding us to grow, learn, and experience Him.

The word *test* makes me break out into a cold sweat as I envision my college days in a sterile classroom with my No. 2 pencil. But we read that God's purpose for testing in Deuteronomy is different from how we understand it: "You shall remember the whole way that the Lord your God has led you these forty years in the wilderness, that He might humble you and test you to *know* what was in your heart" (Deuteronomy 8:2). I've emphasized the word *know* here because I want to explore another layer of meaning we can find by looking closely at the original Hebrew word, *yada*. *Yada* is translated as "know," but it's a knowing that comes from experience. Of course, we know that God is omniscient, so He already knows our hearts, but He also desires to experience our hearts as we experience Him.

The test isn't pass-fail or one we take with our heads down and pencils poised. God's test for the Israelites is designed to help them grow in relationship with and intimate knowledge of Him. It is in the soil of relationship that God uses us to bear His fruit. The wilderness that appears to be a place of death becomes the greenhouse for our growth.

INVITATION

Can you relate to the way the author of Hebrews describes praising God as a sacrifice?

Do you sometimes look at life with God as a pass-fail test? Where is God offering you His grace today?

DAILY BREAD

Look up Galatians 5:16–26. How does God's Spirit offer us freedom? *Walk by the Spirit which is greater than our sinful nature.*
Led by the Spirit

As we just read, the fruit of the Spirit is love, joy, peace, patience, kindness, goodness, faithfulness, gentleness, and self-control. How do you need God to sustain you with His fruit today?

SAY GRACE

Set your mind on things that are above,
not on things that are on earth. For you have died,
and your life is hidden with Christ in God.
(Colossians 3:2–3)

WEEK 6: DAY 4

More than a Rock

My husband and I had just flown from California to Kentucky with our two-year-old son. My hair wasn't the cute "messy hair don't care" tousled style but was truly a disheveled mop. And that was just what I looked like on the outside. On the inside, my nerves were frayed and my soul craved a quiet moment to collect itself. Our toddler had eaten every snack I had packed for the trip, and Nathan and I had been sustained only by airline pretzels.

When we finally checked into our hotel, freshened up, and hit the city streets to look for food, it was 9:30 p.m. We didn't have a car, and every restaurant we passed had closed its kitchen. After we had walked in circles for a mile, my alter ego began to materialize. Let's just say that my alter ego is a hulklike version of my sweet self. It wasn't pretty. I wasn't just grumbling about my circumstances, I was listing all the reasons this situation was my husband's fault—which, of course, it wasn't. My husband—ever-patient—knew that my attacks meant he needed to keep pressing on to find me a hot meal. Finally, we found a restaurant. With a bowl of warm Thai noodles in my belly, I sheepishly apologized to him.

I am ashamed to admit I can turn against the people I love most in my worst moments. Maybe this isn't a story you can relate to, and if that is the case, I could learn something from you! My guess is that many of you have also put your loved ones on trial when things weren't going your way. In that overwhelming moment, it can seem easier to blame others rather than accept difficult circumstances.

This same human reaction happens among the Israelites as they quarrel and blame Moses for their predicament. They accuse, "Why did you bring us up out of Egypt, to kill us and our children and our livestock with thirst?" (Exodus 17:3). Their cries against Moses rise to a crescendo, a full-fledged attack, causing Moses to fear for his life and cry out to God, "What shall I to do with this people? They are almost ready to stone me."

To the Israelites, the crime is that Moses is letting them die of thirst. They are the accusers, and Moses is the accused. They try him in the court of public opinion and want to sentence him to death by stoning. Moses, however, sees that the real transgressors are the Israelites, who doubt and challenge God at every blind bend of their journey.

Jesus Is the Rock

God intervenes and creates a new kind of trial. He tells Moses to bring the elders to the rock at Horeb, where God will stand before them as Moses strikes the rock. The Hebrew word God uses for "strike" is *nåkå*, which can also mean "to scourge" or "to smite." The elders stand witness, and Moses becomes the judge as God takes the punishment that should have been for the Israelites.

> Stricken, smitten, and afflicted,
> See Him dying on the tree
> 'Tis the Christ, by man rejected;
> Yes my soul, 'tis He, 'tis He!
> 'Tis the long-expected Prophet,
> David's Son, yet David's Lord;
> Proofs I see sufficient of it:
> 'Tis the true and faithful Word. (*LSB* 451:1)

In his letter to the Corinthians, Paul affirms that the Rock is Christ.

Write It on Your Heart

Look up 1 Corinthians 10:4.

The guilt and shame we feel after behaving badly toward the people we love most is real and heavy, but there is good news. At Mount Horeb, God demonstrates that Jesus took the punishment we deserved. Water gushes from the rock to quench the thirst of 600,000 men and their families. We know that after Jesus' death on the cross, a Roman soldier pierces Him, and blood and water flow from His side. The forgiveness that comes from Jesus isn't the kind of forgiveness that is doled out little by little or rationed with conditions. Jesus takes the punishment we deserve. From His sacrifice comes the blood of the new covenant that offers us forgiveness and new life in Him. The water reminds us of our Baptism, which is a rebirth into God's family as we receive His grace. The cost is extravagant. God's only Son is our sin offering, which God, our Father, provided; but our prodigal God pays the price so that our needs are met in Him.

The Israelites don't see the whole story, but on that day, they see that God provides. They threaten to stone God's chosen messenger, Moses, because they have no water. But God uses Moses to bring water from a rock. Do they see God's mercy poured out for them despite their sins? In Rephidim, they are invited to a new kind of rest—to rely on the Rock, Christ.

While the Israelites witnessed incredible miracles and walked with God in their midst, today, we understand the miracle of the Rock, Jesus, who was slain for us so we can receive the water that does not run dry. This wilderness world can feel like a daily trial. The accuser launches lies at us: "bad mom," "senile," "fat," "not good enough." In the noise of a needy world and our insufficiency, we can feel abandoned by God. But the stone rolled away from Christ's empty tomb reminds us of God's power in the face of the enemy's empty threats. Every sin that could stone us loses power in Jesus, our Rock, who pardons and provides.

Rock of Ages, cleft for me,

Let me hide myself in Thee;

Let the water and the blood,

From Thy riven side which flowed,

Be of sin the double cure;

Cleanse me from its guilt and pow'r. (*LSB* 761:1)

INVITATION

Where is God inviting you to receive Jesus' forgiveness? Where is He inviting you to offer it?

DAILY BREAD

Look up Galatians 3:10–14. How did Jesus take what we deserved?

Because of the price Jesus paid, what gifts does He give us?

SAY GRACE

Christ, the Rock of our salvation,
Is the name of which we boast;
Lamb of God, for sinners wounded,
Sacrifice to cancel guilt!
None shall ever be confounded
Who on Him their hope have built.
(*LSB* 451:4)

WEEK 6: DAY 5

Living Water

After experiencing betrayal by people I trusted, I felt as if I'd exchanged my innocence for cynicism. Deeply wounded, I no longer approached people with eagerness and openness. Instead, I was just polite enough to get by while I secretly looked at each person's motives with a skeptical side-eye. I justified it, praying, "Okay, God. I really only need a relationship with You. I don't need to be actual friends with anyone else, right?"

During that time, I steeped myself in the rich history and culture of the Old Testament, trying to distance myself from the more emotive parts of the Bible. God used my time in His Word to give me the healing and redirection my heart needed.

God's turbulent relationship with the Israelites isn't only found in the wilderness account. It is found throughout the Old Testament. Again and again, Israel betrays God by turning to idols. Again and again, God forgives them and restores the relationship. The cycle continues, illustrating the impossible gap between God and humankind.

Our sin is the wilderness that blinds and disables us from grabbing hold of God's heart. I was in this wilderness as sin, struggle, disillusionment, deception, and self-doubt layered like sediment on my heart to dull my spiritual senses and disorient my feelings toward God and others. One day, I paused at Jeremiah 31, where the subtitle reads, "The LORD Will Turn Mourning to Joy." Those words felt like God's gentle invitation to step out of the bitterness I had mired myself in.

The promise of restoration I read about in this chapter captured the desire of my heart that I knew was only possible through Jesus. I silently prayed,

Oh, Lord, this hurt is so heavy, I don't want to carry it anymore. My heart longs for joy, but right now, it takes effort to show up. I don't want to feel numb anymore. I need You to put me on the other side of this. Amen.

Have you ever said a prayer like this? Have you ever prayed a prayer of hope that you plant in a barren landscape? A whispered acknowledgment does not have to be the final word on what will be. Has your heart ever become heavy with the weight and loneliness of feeling unknown in a crowded world? As I rested in God's Word, I found hope in Jeremiah's prophetic promise of the coming Messiah. I acknowledged that only the Spirit of God could shift and soften my heart to forgive and trust again. Only God could give me a heart for people and the strength to love them without my human conditions.

As the Holy Spirit heals our hearts of the wounds of abuse, betrayal, loss, and other grief, it is no less a miracle than God using Moses to bring forth water from the rock at Mount Horeb. In this way, we see that trust and forgiveness are central to recognizing God's provision as we walk with Him in the wilderness. His healing comes to us through Jesus' blood and the Holy Spirit, who inspires faith and prompts us to respond to His voice.

We see that Jesus' death, His ascent, and the arrival of the Holy Spirit at Pentecost culminate centuries of prophecy, religious ceremonies, animal sacrifices, history, and tradition. We can look back now and see how the Old Testament points to the arrival of Jesus. But for many Jews and religious leaders, this reality is cloaked in scandal and mystery.

In John 7, as the biblical narrative nears a climax, Jesus attends the Feast of Tabernacles, when the Hebrew people celebrate the gathering of the harvest and gather in tents to remember the exodus from Egypt. At the festival, the religious leaders hunt for Jesus, but He manages to evade them. Then, halfway through the festivities, Jesus begins to teach at the temple courts. On the final day, according to the instruction of the Torah, the priest takes a golden pitcher of water from the pool of Siloam and a silver pitcher of wine and pours it on God's altar as he prays for the coming Messiah. It was then that Jesus proclaims:

Write It on Your Heart

Look up John 7:37.

The water the Israelites drank from the rock at Mount Horeb is a foretaste of the living water we receive through God's Spirit. God's Spirit assures us of our inheritance—eternal life with Him—as He guides us through a fallen world.

A Better View

Not long after the Feast of Tabernacles, Jesus encounters a man born blind. Jesus tells His disciples that his blindness is not a result of anyone's sin "but that the works of God might be displayed in him." Jesus wipes mud made with His saliva over the man's eyes and tells him to wash in the pool of Siloam, where his sight is restored.

Of course, the mud the world throws at us can temporarily blind and disorient us, but God's Spirit cleanses us and reminds us of Jesus' atoning sacrifice. This reality empowers us to trust that Jesus, who went from death to life, is the one who refreshes our hearts and turns our mourning into joy, even as human emotions and painful circumstances threaten to create layers that harden us to others.

The Holy Spirit gives us spiritual senses so we might see and hear, feel and perceive the things of God. Through Jeremiah, God declares a new covenant: "I will put My law within them, and I will write it on their hearts" (Jeremiah 31:33). No longer will they have to tell one another how to follow God, "for they shall all know [Him], from the least of them to the greatest" (Hebrews 8:11). God's promise through Jeremiah has been fulfilled and is being fulfilled in Jesus, who offers us adoption as sons and daughters, making those who were once enemies brothers, sisters, and future heirs of the Father's glory. The Holy Spirit flows from our hardened hearts, and our striving, cynicism, bitterness, and grief soften into trust in Jesus, who forgives and loves. I don't need to understand or justify; I don't need to enable or people please. But I am called to extend the love and forgiveness that comes from God.

Living as People Who Are Sent

Siloam is the Hebrew word for "sent." Just as our Father sent His Son to redeem the world, our Savior sends us as Jesus purifies our hearts with His living water. Believing in Him, He gives us eyes to see where He is sending us. Sometimes God sends us to plant churches in Japan. Sometimes He sends us to extend His love and forgiveness to someone in our local congregation who has hurt us.

Pray: Father, You know the hurt each of us carries. Heal us so that we can bring Your healing to others. Give us a better view of our world through Your eyes. Trade our hearts of stone for hearts of flesh that have Your heartbeat. In Jesus' name. Amen.

When I was working through the hurt in my heart during this difficult season, I wrote something in my journal that I think is worth holding on to today:

> When I want to rage and shake my fist, I remember Jesus loves. When I want to cry, quit, or retaliate, I remember Jesus loves. To follow Him, I remember I am called to love like Him. Sometimes choosing to love others can feel like using mere drops of water to fill an ocean, but I trust He will use every drop. So I don't stop doing what is right, what is good, what is honorable and true in a world thirsty for love. I'll keep using my little watering can.

INVITATION

Where is God sending you to show Jesus' love today?

Can you relate to Lindsay's difficult season? If so, how did the Holy Spirit provide help and healing to you through your difficult time?

DAILY BREAD

Look up John 9:1–11. What is Jesus teaching the man by using mud and sending him to go wash? What is He teaching you with this story?

SAY GRACE

Christ is risen! Grief and sighing,
Sins and sorrows, fall behind;
Fear and failure, doubt, denying,
Full and free forgiveness find.
All the soul's dark night is past,
Morning breaks in joy at last.
(*LSB* 485:4)

WEEK 7

Power through Weakness

For not by their own sword did they win the land,
nor did their own arm save them,
but Your right hand and Your arm,
and the light of Your face,
for You delighted in them.

Psalm 44:3

———

Hidden Power

Have you ever played tug-of-war? I've played it once, reluctantly, during a college retreat. A puddle of mud was in the middle, which meant the stakes were high. People rallied on either side of the rope. Not wanting to get muddy, I picked the side with the burliest-looking guys. The whistle blew, and I pulled and pulled as the other team inched toward us. I leaned my body back and yanked with every God-given muscle I had, confident that my efforts were essential to our team's progress. When I eventually ran out of strength to grip the rope, I released it for a second of rest. Right at that moment, with a collective grunt, a herculean yank, and a whoop of victory, the other team toppled toward us into the mud. I staggered out of the fray, recognizing that my 120-pound body and minuscule muscles didn't even tip the balance. The victory was ours—without my help.

Our own strength is minuscule as God works through us to accomplish His purposes. We don't even tip the balance when it comes to our brawn. God doesn't seek out leaders for their military prowess, political connections, influencer status, or the number of degrees they have. Instead, God seeks men and women who are humble, obedient, seek His heart, and submit themselves to Him. Enter Moses.

Moses is alive only because of God's protection. Pharaoh had ordered all Hebrew sons under age 2 to be cast into the Nile River to die. But Moses' mother keeps him alive in secret until he is three months old. Then she puts him in a basket, placing him "among the reeds on the riverbank" (Exodus 2:3), where Pharaoh's daughter finds him and takes pity on him.

Through this God-orchestrated rescue, Moses is protected and grows up in the Egyptian court.

When Moses sees the unjust way Pharaoh treats the Hebrew people, he tries to take justice in his own hands. He kills an Egyptian he had seen beating a Hebrew. When word gets out, Moses flees to Midian, where he marries a Midianite woman and begins a new life as a shepherd. Moses' future appears pretty mapped out. Moses is nearly eighty when God times things just right to redirect Moses' mission for His purposes.

You probably know about the famous exchange between Moses and God at the burning bush, but if you need a refresher, read Exodus 3–4. Here is a brief recap: Moses encounters God in the burning bush and then does everything he can to shirk the assignment God asks of him. God meets each of Moses' excuses with signs, wisdom, and grace. Then God commands Moses to take his staff, which he would use to perform signs, and return to Egypt. In short order, Moses and his brother, Aaron, go to the Egyptian court and say to Pharaoh, "Thus says the LORD, the God of Israel, 'Let My people go, that they may hold a feast to Me in the wilderness'" (Exodus 5:1).

Has God ever redirected your plans for His purposes? Have you been challenged to do something that feels beyond your capabilities and calling? In that critical moment at the burning bush, Moses faces his own wilderness. He needs to recognize his past mistakes and confused identity. God commands Moses to walk straight back into the struggle he ran from forty years ago. Then he will face his past with God's strength and more. God will guide him to a better future.

A New Battle

The next story we encounter in our journey through Exodus is the battle of Rephidim, where the Israelites face more struggle and opposition in the wilderness. Last week, we looked at how Moses struck the rock and God provided water for the whole community. But on the heels of this miracle, the Amalekites, a disreputable desert gang, attack the Israelites.

The Israelites had been whining about food and water, and now they face another threat they are even less prepared to handle. Moses is advanced in years and leads a nation of former slaves trained to make bricks, not warriors trained for combat. When the Egyptians pursue the Israelites, God gives them an escape and defeats their enemy. But this time, the Israelites are being challenged to face their enemies in battle. The odds are stacked against them as they are surrounded, but Moses and the Israelites have God on their side.

In the Book of 2 Kings, the Assyrian king sends an army to surround the city to seize the prophet Elisha. Overwhelmed and afraid, Elisha's servant cries, "What shall we do?" Elisha responds, "Don't be afraid . . . those who are with us are more than those who are with them" (6:15–16). Elisha sees another reality. He prays, and the Lord opens the servant's eyes to take in the hillside filled with angel armies positioned for their defense.

Just as God's unseen power is revealed to Elisha's servant, His power is demonstrated through Moses and Israel as they take on the Amalekites.

At the battle of Rephidim, a different perspective of God's power is displayed as Moses sends Joshua into battle and stands on the hill to hold God's staff aloft, securing an unlikely victory.

We'll spend more time this week looking at this story, but today, let's take a moment to look at how we can rest in God's power at work in our own lives.

This week in the wilderness, is there somewhere you want to remember God's unseen

---

Activities to Rest and Remember

- Read God's Word.
- Listen to worship music.
- Pray the Psalms.
- Take a walk and pay attention to God's creation.
- Think of all the ways God has provided for you today and throughout your lifetime.
- Call a friend and pray together.

power at work in your life? Write it down as a reminder.

We can remember:

Those who are with us _____ _____ _____

those who are with them. (2 Kings 6:16)

God's power can change the outcome of wars and cause the rise and fall of nations. The power that raised Jesus from the dead is working in each of us through the Holy Spirit. If you feel out of your league or at the end of your strength and solutions, God invites you to surrender. His power works best in our weakness.

Sometimes my life can feel like an exhausting game of tug-of-war as I use all my strength to keep things from going into the proverbial mud pit (especially my house)! If you're clutching tightly to the rope of your life, yanking, pulling, huffing, and puffing to keep everything moving forward, would you take a moment with me and release it? Let's pause and remember that God's strength is sufficient.

INVITATION

Have you been trying to overcome or solve a problem on your own?

How is the Holy Spirit inviting you to let go?

DAILY BREAD

Look up Ephesians 1:15–23. What is the purpose of Paul's prayer for the Ephesians? How is it important for the church today?

SAY GRACE

But thanks be to God, who gives us the victory through our Lord Jesus Christ. (1 Corinthians 15:57)

Renewed Strength

It was a graveyard of defective toys. One by one, my two-year-old son took each broken toy, collected like lost things in the bottom of his toy chest, and laid them before me. He said, "Broken." But it just meant that I needed to buy batteries. I ruefully began the task of writing down the various batteries I would need to order.

I inspected each item, including a turtle that was supposed to teach letters and numbers, a police car that was supposed to make a siren sound and flash its lights, and remote controls that were now useless blocks with antennas. Each toy was disempowered, no longer able to do the thing it had been designed to do.

Do you ever feel like you are just going through the motions, living a life that feels void of power and purpose? How often do we keep going, running on empty toward something we don't clearly see or understand? We plan and push, perform and prove that we are capable, qualified, and purposeful, only to reach the end of our energy and capacity and come up against a brick wall emblazoned with the words "I don't know" or, worse, "I don't care anymore." We can sidestep our insufficiency; we can even pretend for a while that we know what we're doing. But sooner or later, each of us will come to the end of ourselves.

The end of our knowledge.

The end of our patience.

The end of our strength.

The end of our resources.

The end of our energy.

We come to the end of our influence, power, or vision for the future.

Do you remember the account of Jesus healing the blind man at the pool of Siloam that we looked at last week? When the man reports the event to the religious leaders, they tell him that Jesus is not from God. The blind man responds, "If this man were not from God, He could do nothing" (John 9:33). Jesus, God in flesh, can do all things but came to fulfill Scripture, including, "to proclaim good news to the poor" to "proclaim liberty to the captives and recovering of sight to the blind, to set at liberty those who are oppressed" (Luke 4:18).

Hearing about this man's mission to witness to the healing power of Jesus makes me wonder if there is a specific purpose He calls each of us to fulfill. Like the lifeless toy turtle with powerless buttons or the mute plastic blocks that were once remote controls, we face our own powerlessness at some point in our lives. Striving for energy and purpose without God's power leads to disillusionment and burnout. Or we can begin to think that striving is what God wants from us. Tired and cranky with little visible results, we can become frustrated, throwing up our hands and proclaiming, "God, do You see how hard I'm working down here?!"

As we talked about on day one of this week, Moses learns about doing things on his own the hard way. His own plan sets him back forty years and sends him on a long sabbatical in the desert. Nevertheless, Moses is the perfect example of how God redeems and empowers us for His purposes. But that doesn't mean it's an easy journey. As we talk about the Israelites' wilderness journey, let's give Moses some extra consideration as he navigates his own wilderness and God shapes him into a prophet, leader, and man of God.

It's one thing to recognize that the Israelites are stumbling through the wilderness, grumbling, fumbling, and complaining. But we might assume that everything comes easily to Moses. He is humble, God loves him, and he is constantly pointing the Israelites to a better perspective of God. Unlike other Old Testament prophets, Moses speaks with God face-to-face as one speaks to a friend (see Exodus 33). Moses is certainly an exalted prophet God uses to do critical work, but it's also important to recognize that he is a fallen human. Moses faces moments of fear (see Exodus 2), doubt and insecurity (see Exodus 4), and anger (see Numbers 20). He is challenged to walk through his own wilderness, where God shapes his identity and character. God doesn't just create opportunities for the Israelites to grow in faith and trust in God, He also develops Moses into the leader God needs him to be for the Israelites.

In Rephidim, Moses again faces the reality of an enemy attack. But this time, he responds decisively, dispatching Joshua to lead the rag-tag Israelite army into an unfair fight against the battle-ready Amalekites. Moses climbs up a hill and raises his arms to hold the staff of God aloft. Then something unexpected happens. When he raises his arms with the staff, the Israelite army has a breakthrough in the battle. But when he lowers his arms to rest, the Amalekites gain ground. Moses is learning through real-time experience about God's game-changing power. Moses gets a picture of how God partners with His people in prayer. God uses the staff as an instrument to channel His power for victory through Moses' intercession.

Try-Hard Life or Life of Trust?

Where is your power source in this wilderness season? You may already know that the only thing sustaining you through the day is the Holy Spirit, who gives you enough strength for the moment. But if this question leads you to consider if you are completing this journey on your own, then friend, you are not alone. I am awesome at the try-hard life. My identity comes from my performance, and my value comes from looking good to everyone around me, even though my soul is hollering for help. In this place, Jesus reaches out to me and calls me back to a life of rest in Him.

Is He reaching His hand out to you right now? Surrender is the most challenging and boldest thing we can do as an act of defiance in a world bent on self-reliance. It is in surrender that we realize our purpose in God's kingdom. We were not made to impress, please, and squeeze into a man-made image of success. As we take a step back from the ongoing battle of life, we reach up to heaven for His will to be done on earth.

Pray: Father, You invite us to pray, "Thy will be done on earth as it is in heaven." We pray that You would give us faith to hope in Your power, which brings justice on earth. As grown-ups, we are weighed down with more responsibility and a sense of powerlessness. We face circumstances that are out of our control. Remind us of our identity as Your children, invited to rest in Your strength as we face the wilderness where You shape us to be more like Your Son. In Jesus' name. Amen.

INVITATION

Have you experienced God's supernatural power at work in your circumstances? Share your experience.

Where do you need God's power in your circumstances today?

DAILY BREAD

Look up John 9:11–33. What is the difference between the power that the Pharisees exercise versus the power that Jesus demonstrates?

SAY GRACE

Give thanks to the Lord, for He is good,
for His steadfast love endures forever. (Psalm 136:1)

WEEK 7: DAY 3

Power in Prayer

"Sometimes all we can do is pray," said the old man as he sat in the hospital cafeteria. He stared into the mug of black coffee he held between his hands like a Magic 8 Ball. But the answers he waited for were not within reach. From one table away, I sipped my coffee and listened as he recounted stories of past procedures and surgeries, like ebenezers, that marked his wife's difficult health journey. He said this was supposed to be her final surgery, with cautious hope. Three hours had passed since his wife had entered the operating room, but he waited with an alertness that suggested that news would come at any minute.

When part of your heart is rolled away on a stretcher, out of reach and out of sight, you reckon with your helplessness. Even if you're not the type of person who prays, faced with the alternative of doing nothing, many stumble into a conversation with God.

I had my own moment of need in that same hospital when my then five-month-old son Boe was sick with RSV. He was connected to oxygen and a feeding tube. I had a prayer chain that stretched from California to Delaware. My new friend from the cafeteria was right: sometimes all we can do is pray. But too often we see prayer as resignation rather than remembering God's power and breakthrough available through prayer.

Moses demonstrates that prayer is a critical part of our battle strategy in the face of an enemy attack. Although only God has the power to change the outcome, He looks for us to humble ourselves before Him and request what we need.

Write It on Your Heart

Look up 2 Chronicles 7:14. *If my people who are called by My name will humble themselves & pray and seek My face & turn from their evil ways, then will I hear from heaven & will forgive their sin & heal their land.*

I don't know what happened to the man in the cafeteria. I don't know how the surgery went for his wife. But for a few minutes, I could shoulder some of the weight of his grief and anxiety. Our good-bye came quicker than I would have liked, and as I left him, my heart was unsettled, knowing we aren't supposed to face these kinds of difficult battles alone.

That was also true for Moses at the battle of Rephidim when he receives support in prayer from his brother, Aaron, and his friend Hur:

But Moses' hands grew weary, so they took a stone and put it under him, and he sat on it, while Aaron and Hur held up his hands, one on one side, and the other on the other side. (Exodus 17:12)

As Moses travels through his own wilderness, he is learning the power of prayer and that he needs other faithful people by his side. Our triune God's very identity is relational as Father, Son, and Holy Spirit. On that hill, overlooking the battle, Moses is invited to model surrender. Those men place a rock for him to sit on and then stand beside him to hold up his arms.

When we are weary from battle in our wilderness times, we can rest on the Rock, Jesus. In Jesus, our eternal victory is already secure, but we are invited to be intimately involved in God's strategy for the moment-to-moment battles of everyday life. Yes, our prayers can change the tide of events. That happens when Moses lifts his staff and Israel gains ground and again when he lowers his arms and the Israelites are pushed back by the Amalekites. But as Moses grows tired, he quickly learns that he cannot win the battle of intercession alone. It is only with the help of his trusted brothers supporting him as he prays that God would bring the victory.

Prayer People

It is tempting to want to get through the challenges in life alone. But in those moments when we are faced with the reality that "all we can do is pray," there is comfort and hope in knowing that we are not praying alone.

What are the names of the people on your prayer team? For those of you who feel unsure, I invite you to write a prayer to God below, asking that He would bring those people into your life or reveal to you who they are.

Next, ask yourself who you can stand beside to strengthen through intercessory prayer? We have the privilege to pray "at all times in the Spirit, with all prayer and supplication," as we make "supplication for all the saints" (Ephesians 6:18).

Take a moment to write the names God is putting on your heart now.

When "all we can do is pray," God invites us to recognize that prayer is not just the lifeline but His design for us as we walk with Him through this wilderness life. When our brothers and sisters are too weak to whisper anything more than "help me, Jesus," we lift their arms with ours and cry, "Not by might, nor power, but by My Spirit, says the LORD of hosts" (Zechariah 4:6). By the power of God's Spirit, Moses sets the Israelites free from slavery. Still, Jesus, "counted worthy of more glory than Moses," has set us free from sin and death (Hebrews 3:3). As we sit in the wilderness of a fallen world, we ask our Father to turn the tide of our difficult circumstances.

Sitting for three days in my son's hospital room, all I could do was pray and wait. Friends took turns sitting beside his bed, eyeing his oxygen level and whispering prayers so I could get a couple hours of rest. Boe's nurse held my hand as we prayed for his healing. And in time, God answered.

MORNING SONG

O   a w a k e,   **sleeping sons,**   daughters   arise;

look

squint your eyes   **to the dawn ;** yes drink in the light

Jesus is upon

the wilderness past   **u s,**   darkness no m o r e;

you

you   **knew it believed it, that this life meant**   more;

There is NO MORE DEATH

b u t   **now your hope realized, your heart** is secure

a new creation

children of   light   **c o m e,** infants on h i p s;

receive His

walls   o f   **salvation,** praise on our lips

Kingdom

gates   are   **open,**   mouths open wide,

the veil torn

no longer hungry, **our Lord.**   s a t i s f i e s;

victorious

n o w   y o u   **behold Him,** God's g l o r y arise

death

no more mourning,   **n o w**   it's m o r n i n g,

no more

tears wiped from our eyes.

Poem by Lindsay Hausch[14]

One day, Boe was attached to tubes and barely alert, and twelve hours later, he was off the machines and bright-eyed.

Sometimes all we can do is pray. That is more than enough. Our banner of surrender becomes God's banner over us.

INVITATION

Is God inviting you to see prayer from a new perspective? How will you respond?

DAILY BREAD

Look up Acts 1:12–14. What picture of the Early Church is Paul illustrating? Is this a reality in your life? If not, what is a step you can take to live this out today? *praying together with other believers*

SAY GRACE

I do not cease to give thanks for you,
remembering you in my prayers. (Ephesians 1:16)

WEEK 7: DAY 4

Jesus in the Wilderness

After Jesus is baptized in the Jordan River, He enters the wilderness where He resists Satan's temptation for forty days. Ultimately, in His trial and death, Jesus faces the greatest wilderness the world has ever known.

Our loving Jesus kneels at the Mount of Olives and begs our Father to take away the suffering He knows is ahead of Him. His disciples, just a stone's throw away, sleep deeply in their exhaustion, unaware of Jesus' desperate need for His brothers to stand beside Him. Because of the torment in His soul, Jesus prays so intensely that He sweats drops of blood. But even in His dark night of the soul, Jesus, in perfect submission and obedience, prays, "Not My will, but Yours, be done" (Luke 22:42).

The next day, stripped and beaten, Jesus will spread His arms out before a mocking crowd and take on all the punishment for sin that humankind deserves. But the physical torment will be only a piece of His suffering. In His moment of greatest need, Jesus' greatest anguish is when He is completely cut off from His Father and the intimate communion He has known since the beginning of time. Jesus is about to accomplish what none of us can ever achieve in life: "canceling the record of debt that stood against us with its legal demands" (Colossians 2:14). He crushes Satan, sin, and darkness, "disarm[ing] all rulers and authorities" (Colossians 2:14–15). Through the crushing of His own body, Jesus makes new wine for us to drink from the cup of forgiveness.

But His mission doesn't stop with His last excruciating breaths on the cross. In three days, Jesus reveals God's power over death itself. As God raises Him from the dead, Jesus becomes the better manna, the bread of life from heaven, so that anyone "may eat of it and not die" but have the promise of eternal life with Him (John 6:51).

Moses' battle plan at Rephidim aligns with Jesus' battle victory at the cross and tomb. Both Moses and Jesus find strength and breakthroughs in absolute surrender to the authority of the Father. Wielding Yahweh's staff and rod, Moses, through God's strength, rescues God's people from slavery and injustice. The staff is a powerful reminder to Moses and all Israel that Yahweh is the source of power. Jesus comes in the flesh to open the path to freedom from sin. He lives in complete obedience to the Father. He tells the Jews who question Him for performing miracles on the Sabbath, "My Father is working until now, I am working. . . . The Son can do nothing of His own accord, but only what He sees the Father doing" (John 5:17, 19).

Just as Moses uses a staff to guide God's people, the Bible illustrates Jesus as a shepherd. David prophetically writes about Jesus' staff and rod in Psalm 23: "I will fear no evil, for You are with me; Your rod and Your staff, they comfort me" (v. 4). We know what the staff is, but what is the rod? In the Book of Revelation, John also mentions Jesus having a rod of iron (see Revelation 2:26). As menacing as it sounds, while the staff guides sheep, the rod was used by shepherds to protect their sheep from predators. In this light, the staff and rod point to God's ultimate battle plan to save and protect His people through Jesus, our Good Shepherd.

Write It on Your Heart

Look up Isaiah 53:6. *We all, like sheep, have gone astray, each of us has gone his own way; and the Lord has laid on him the iniquity of us all.*

The Cross Is Our Banner

The staff held aloft by Moses also points to Jesus' cross. He is raised up to achieve victory. Just as a wooden cross and nails gain meaning through God's sovereign will, the staff and rod Moses and Aaron use throughout the wilderness journey are not the sources of power but are God's props in His divine plan to point people to Jesus.

After the Israelites gain victory over the Amalekites, Moses builds an altar and calls it Yahweh-Nissi, meaning "the Lord is my banner" (Exodus 17:15). Soldiers use banners in war to mark where their commander is. Just as soldiers need to be able to see and know where their commander is for directives, the people of Israel are learning that they need to look to God for direction. God is their provision for daily needs and their protection from enemies.

For Christians today, the cross is our banner. When soldiers are in battle, they can grow fatigued and disoriented. In the unexpected attacks that blind us and the nonstop noise of our lives, it can be easy to lose focus and sight of our purpose. But Jesus never lost sight of His purpose on earth. God's breath, which created man, became labored breaths as He died a man's most humiliating death. Jesus' hands are held aloft by nails on a cross in surrender. But in His absolute surrender, Jesus breathes again in victory over death.

Pray: Father, we pray that You would show us the crosses You call us to carry, knowing the victory is ours in Jesus. Give us hope in Your resurrection power in our wilderness struggles as we remember that by Jesus' wounds, we are healed. In His name. Amen.

As we face our human weakness, we can look to Jesus, who demonstrates the power that doesn't just overcome weakness but comes through weakness. The wilderness becomes a place where we are invited to gaze at the wounds of Jesus as we embrace the divine struggle that is our ultimate healing.

INVITATION

Where is God inviting you to take up your cross and follow Him today?

DAILY BREAD

Look up Hebrews 13:20–21. Who is at the center of this verse? How does that impact us in the wilderness of our lives today?

May the God of peace, who through the blood of the eternal covenant brought back from the dead our Lord Jesus, that great Shepherd of the sheep equip you with everything good for doing His will & may He work in us what is pleasing to Him

SAY GRACE

I will give thanks to the LORD with my whole heart;
I will recount all of Your wonderful deeds.

(Psalm 9:1)

The Justice of the Cross

God's justice is a prominent theme in the Old Testament. It can be hard to get our heads around that fact. How is God all loving and fully just at the same time? And how do we reconcile that with how He chooses to exact punishment? After the Israelites defeat the Amalekites at Rephidim, God tells Moses to "write this as a memorial in a book and recite it in the ears of Joshua, that I will utterly blot out the memory of Amalek from under heaven" (Exodus 17:14).

Since we know God embodies love and justice simultaneously, we embrace that His perfect love is also the lens through which He defines justice. His justice is the outreaching of His love—the two intertwined in a divine paradigm that invites us to our knees in worship. As we confess our limited understanding, embracing a posture before God's feet, we take a closer look at the lessons God is unfolding through this complicated story.

At the battle of Rephidim, the Amalekites are defeated but aren't wiped out entirely. A Google search pointed me to all the places the Amalekites resurfaced in the Old Testament. Every time we encounter them, they are stealing from, killing, and overcoming God's people.

About four hundred years after Israel's first victory in the wilderness, King Saul loses his anointing as king of Israel because of the Amalekites. King Saul doesn't follow God's instruction from the prophet Samuel to destroy the Amalekites and everything that belongs to them, including their cattle. Instead, Saul saves the choice cattle and takes King Agag, the Amalekite king, as a captive. Samuel confronts him, and Saul confesses his sin and begs Samuel to change the verdict. But God had made up His mind. He will appoint another man to be king of Israel. Samuel executes King Agag himself, saying, "As your sword has made women childless, so shall your mother be childless among women" (1 Samuel 15:33).

God takes His demand to remove all of Amalek's descendants from the face of the earth very seriously. So seriously, His instruction includes the destruction of even their animals. But why? A trip to the Book of Deuteronomy, where Moses tells the Israelites God's instructions for them, gives us more insight:

> Remember what Amalek did to you on the way as you came out of Egypt, how he attacked you on the way when you were faint and weary, and cut off your tail, those who were lagging behind you, and he did not fear God. Therefore when the LORD your God is giving you for an inheritance to possess, you shall blot out the memory of Amalek from under heaven; you shall not forget. (Deuteronomy 25:17–19)

Rather than attack the Israelites head-on, the Amalekites infiltrate from the back of the camp, meaning they prey upon the sick, pregnant, elderly, or young. Amalek doesn't fear God; he is motivated only to satisfy his hunger for wealth and power, reminding us of another enemy of Israel: Pharaoh.

We started the week by looking at Moses' early life in Egypt. He tries to take justice into his own hands by killing an Egyptian for mistreating a Hebrew. This is in direct contrast to God's justice, as Jesus' brother, James, tells us, "The anger of man does not produce the righteousness of God" (James 1:20). God brings justice as we submit ourselves to Him rather than to the whims of our human emotions.

In Egypt, when Moses confronted Pharaoh and God brought the ten plagues, Moses was still learning how God's justice operates. He grasped the magnitude of God's power at the Red Sea as the Israelites safely escaped from the Egyptian army, which was swept into the sea. At Rephidim, Moses doesn't hesitate. He gives a decisive battle plan, sending Joshua and Israel's fittest men to fight.

He designates himself as the conduit of God's power. Moses learns that justice comes from God alone.

As we discussed on day four of this week, God uses Moses and Aaron to perform many signs and wonders with their staffs throughout the Book of Exodus, reminding us of Jesus, our Good Shepherd. But it may come as a surprise to learn that Pharaoh is also famous for having a shepherd's staff, known as his crook. Pharaoh's crook speaks of his ultimate power and dominion over the Egyptian people. Pharaoh holds the position of dictator over Egypt. If you look at images depicting ancient Egyptian pharaohs, you may see them with a crook in their hands. Pharaoh's crook speaks of his imposed power and position. In contrast, Aaron's and Moses' staffs point to God's sovereign power and provision as He guides and provides for the Israelites through the wilderness. God uses Moses' and Aaron's staffs as symbols and tools to remind them of God's supernatural reality in the face of this world's limitations, scarcity, and oppression.

Pharaoh's crook speaks of his *imposed* *power* and *position*.

Aaron's and Moses' staffs points to God's *sovereign* *power* and *provision*.

Just as we fall into the temptation to bring about justice on our terms, we often try to impose our own will on others, using the weight of our power, credentials, or other human achievements. As we look at the contrast between the crook and the staff, we are invited to surrender our human will to trust in God's sovereign will.

How is God inviting you to release your power and trust God's will in your wilderness today?

Blotting Out Sin

We look for justice in presidential candidates, government officials, or political parties. We can even get lost looking for justice in good places, like food pantries, homeless shelters, or social movements. But we might forget that God belongs at the center. God desires to use us to bring His love and justice to our world through our prayers, work, big dreams, and small actions. In this life, we look for value, justice, purpose, and power from God alone, trusting that His ways are better.

The Amalekites demonstrate the sin and lawlessness that exist in our world due to the fall. Our just God didn't just defeat the Amalekites in a single battle. He ultimately eliminates the name of Amalek to stop their destruction on earth. In the same way, the Father sends Jesus to blot out sin and the death and destruction it causes, accomplished only by Jesus' total surrender to the will of His Father through His death on the cross.

The ultimate recipient of the world's brokenness, Jesus, allows His body to be broken to bring healing and restoration. In a world where injustices like prejudice, abuse, violence, and oppression are endemic, it is easy to become angry, bitter, or self-righteous. But Jesus shows us the path of self-sacrifice, humility, and love. The world's injustices are overwhelming and demoralizing. Our lives are hard enough, so how can we walk the path of Jesus? We are unable to face the enemy on our own, but read what Paul reminds us.

Write It on Your Heart

Look up Philippians 4:13. *I can do everything through him who gives me strength.*

When we are not enough, we look to Jesus, who demonstrates His perfect love, which brings justice. It seems small, like a baby born in a manger, a king on a donkey, or a criminal's death, but in the kingdom of God, slow is fast and small is big. We look to Jesus, who gives us vision, time, and His grace to do small things with great love that change the world.

INVITATION

How is God's definition of justice different from how the world defines justice? How does this invite you to respond?

DAILY BREAD

Read Matthew 25:31–40. How does God call us to bring about His justice in our world? *deeds of mercy serve without thought of reward God's work of blessing from creation continued in history + was active in the worship + life of His people*

How does this help you embrace the circumstances God has placed you in today?

SAY GRACE

Both riches and honor come from You, and You
rule over all. In Your hand are power and might, and in
Your hand it is to make great and to give strength to all.
And now we thank You, our God, and praise
Your glorious name. (1 Chronicles 29:12–13)

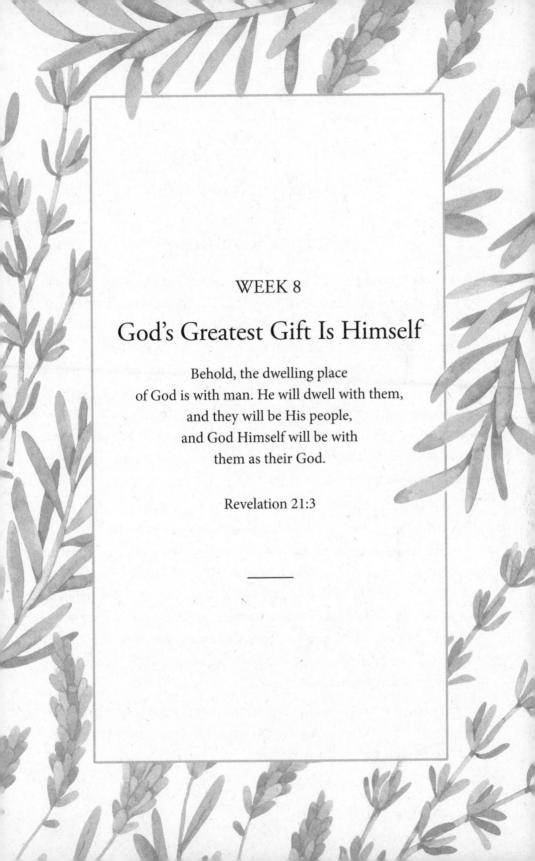

WEEK 8

God's Greatest Gift Is Himself

Behold, the dwelling place
of God is with man. He will dwell with them,
and they will be His people,
and God Himself will be with
them as their God.

Revelation 21:3

———

WEEK 8: DAY 1

Fear or Wonder

Mr. Von's Spanish class wasn't easy. He had high expectations, and even the students who would goof off in other classes were on their best behavior for him. When we didn't meet his expectations, he'd let us know. And we knew what he really cared about was not so much our Spanish skills but who we were as people. Sure, there were teachers in our school who gave easy A's and no homework—their only expectation was that we showed up—but those weren't the teachers who had kids hanging back after the bell rang to talk with them. Mr. Von did. We knew he respected us, and that earned our respect. He challenged us to be the kind of people who would make him proud.

I'm sure as I share this, a teacher or respected adult from your past comes to mind. Maybe they never told you how much they cared, but they showed it by consistently being available and by seeing more in you than you ever saw in yourself. If you were the kid who colored outside the lines, did you have a loving adult to encourage your creativity? If you were one to always follow every rule, did you have a compassionate adult who appreciated your efforts? As you hit puberty and your maturing body felt too clunky for your childlike heart, did someone take time to see past your awkwardness and uncertainty?

God is the Israelites' loving Father and Teacher. He sees them as His treasure. In our reading today, God's promise to Moses is fulfilled as the Israelites approach Mount Sinai.

At the burning bush, He tells Moses, "This shall be the sign for you . . . when you have brought the people out of Egypt, you shall serve God on this mountain" (Exodus 3:12).

As they set up camp in the wilderness of Sinai, I imagine Moses' head starts spinning with wonder at all that has happened since the last time he was with God at Mount Sinai. God has delivered the Israelites from the oppression of the Egyptians, provides for them in extraordinary ways, and delivers them safely to serve Him in the wilderness. Until this point in their journey, God has continually guided and provided for the Israelites, showing them compassion and forgiveness in response to their doubting and complaining. He has asked nothing of them except that they follow and trust Him. But at Mount Sinai, God desires so much more for Moses and His people. He wants to enter into a covenant relationship with the Israelites.

A covenant is a mutual agreement between two parties. The Latin root *convenire* means "to come together, agree."[11] The Hebrew people referred to it as "cutting a covenant" because the alliance was established by killing and cutting an animal—giving the idiom "cutting a deal" a whole new meaning! But the covenant between God and the Israelite people is not an equal agreement. Our omnipotent God, full of mercy and love, with storehouses of blessing, wants a relationship with imperfect humans. He asks only that they obey and worship Him alone:

> You yourselves have seen what I did to the Egyptians, and how I bore you on eagles' wings and brought you to Myself. Now therefore, if you will indeed obey My voice and keep My covenant, you shall be My treasured possession among all peoples, for all the earth is mine. (Exodus 19:4–5)

This seems like it is pretty straightforward. God is offering His people a life of favor and blessing, so it should be a happily ever after. But as you know, it gets a bit dicey. God tells Moses to have the people prepare for His presence to come to Mount Sinai. The people consecrate themselves through ceremonial washing and sexual abstinence, and Moses creates a barrier surrounding the mountain that the people can't pass. On the third day, there is thunder and lightning with loud trumpet blasts, and God descends on the mountain in fire. The people tremble as Moses brings them out to stand at the foot of the mountain and meet God, where He delivers the Commandments to the Israelites. But this is all too much for God's chosen people. Their fear of God's majesty makes them want to retreat. They say to Moses, "You speak to us, and we will listen; but do not let God speak to us, lest we die" (20:19).

I get where the Israelites are coming from. "Lightning, fire, and trumpets? God, why don't You descend in the form of a gentle shepherd and offer them a nice cup of chamomile tea? Yes, God, a softer approach may be just the ticket!"

But God is after something more from the Israelites than just their comfort. He is actually trying to instill fear in them, as Moses explains: "God has come to test you, that the fear of Him may be before you, that you may not sin" (20:20).

Wait. If we're reading this right, God wants them to be afraid? Yes. And no. The nuances of the Hebrew language offer us insight into the text's more profound message. While the English language indicates fear is a lack of trust, with synonyms such as *dread* and *terror*, the Hebrew word *yir'ah* has a broader range of meanings, from the negative experience of fright to the more positive sense of respect, reverence, and awe.

God isn't a distant leader with low expectations and little interest. He wants to inspire healthy fear that shapes the Israelites into His holy people. He wants to transform them into "a kingdom of priests and a holy nation" (19:6). In this light, this is the kind of fear we want to experience.

How is God inviting you into a different, healthier fear of Him? Just as I hope you have experienced the blessing of a positive role model, I'm guessing you might also know the damage an authority figure who abused power can do. These unhealthy relationships can interfere with our understanding of God. I invite you to pray that God would highlight the lies that you believe about Him and replace them with the truth of who He is.

Our God is just and righteous, but He is also gentle and merciful.

Throughout Scripture, when we see the fear that evokes reverence, it is written as *yir'at Yahweh*, or "the fear of the LORD."

The *fear of the LORD* is a fountain of life, that one may turn away from the snares of death. (Proverbs 14:27, emphasis added)

The *fear of the LORD* is the beginning of wisdom; all those who practice it have a good understanding. His praise endures forever! (Psalm 111:10, emphasis added)

The fear of the Lord is grounded in His love and mercy, which create transformation. This transformation doesn't happen with stiff-necked rules or power struggles but through sacrificial love that draws close to us.

The God of Mount Sinai who appears before His people and invites them into a covenant relationship is the same God we know today. But because we can't meet our end of the agreement, God creates a new covenant through His Son, Jesus. The same God who appears in fire and lightning, shaking mountains and parting seas, comes to us as a helpless baby, a humble man, a Suffering Servant, and our Teacher.

Write It on Your Heart

Look up Romans 5:8. *But God demonstrates His own love for us in this: While we were still sinners, Christ died for us*

Through Jesus, we come near to God in the quiet places to pray instead of a dark and quaking mountain. As children of the promise, through faith in Jesus, we understand that the greatest wilderness is separation from God. In light of this reality, the promised land of heaven becomes a person instead of a place. As we approach Mount Zion and enter the city of the living God, our trembling turns to praise. The distance between our wilderness and God's promises gains new meaning as we see behind the veil.

INVITATION

Has your understanding of the "fear of the Lord" shifted? Why or why not?

DAILY BREAD

Look up Exodus 19:14–25 and Hebrews 12:18–24. How are these scenes different? Through the blood of Jesus, how are we invited to approach God today?

SAY GRACE

In God we have boasted continually,
and we will give thanks to Your name forever.

(Psalm 44:8)

Law or Blessing?

At the beginning of the account of the exodus, we are introduced to a new generation of Israelites who are enslaved, worked ruthlessly, and oppressed by Pharaoh. God hears their anguished cries and dispatches His messengers, Moses and Aaron, to assert God's rightful ownership. They tell Pharaoh, "Thus says the LORD, 'Let My people go, that they may serve Me'" (Exodus 8:1). But getting the people out of Egypt is only the first step. In the wilderness, God removes Egypt from the Israelites' hearts and seeks to give them new hearts that beat for Him.

In the ancient Near East, it was common to tattoo or brand servants who were enslaved to a master or deity. Men and women dedicated to service in a temple would get tattoos that symbolized the god they served. But God's chosen people are to be set apart differently. Yahweh doesn't simply desire an external mark but an internal transformation that comes only through a covenant relationship with Him. Later, God instructs Joshua to circumcise the Israelites once they enter the Promised Land to honor the covenant He made with Abraham (see Genesis 17:10). Ultimately, though, God wants more than a physical circumcision; He wants a circumcision of the heart.

Write It on Your Heart

Look up Deuteronomy 10:16. *Circumcise your hearts therefore and do not be stiff necked any longer*

In the new covenant, through Jesus, our Baptism replaces circumcision. We receive a circumcision of the heart "made without hands," where the Spirit of God cuts away our sinful nature (Colossians 2:11). This means the Law is not the means for a right relationship with God but an invitation to living a life that honors Him.

Too often, we look at the Mosaic Law as something that confines the Israelites rather than the means to a life of greater freedom with God. In Jesus' time, the religious elite had made the Law their master, but that was never God's design. It is important to look at the Law through the broader lens of the exodus account. God has just delivered the Israelites from slavery! He has cared for them through their wilderness journey and delivered them from their enemies. Then He wants to give them a covenant so He can bless them. God's Law guides them on how they can flourish and represent His name well to other nations.

An acrostic poem, Psalm 119 is notable for many reasons. It is the longest psalm and is written in the order of the Hebrew alphabet. But there's more. Rather than just a portrait of someone who is a student of the Law or resignedly follows it out of obligation, it paints a picture of someone who experiences joy and transformation by walking with God as he seeks to follow His commands.

> Blessed are those whose way is blameless,
>   who walk in the law of the LORD!
> Blessed are those who keep His testimonies,
>   who seek Him with their whole heart,
> who also do no wrong,
>   but walk in His ways! (Psalm 119:1–3)

While Pharaoh demands the slaughter of their sons, unflinching loyalty, and back-breaking labor, the God of the Israelites, through His Law, demonstrates that His kingdom and His ways look nothing like the sinful world. Through what He stands against—idolatry, adultery, jealousy, theft, murder, and more—God is declaring that He is set apart, a God of life who cares about the hearts and lives of each person.

More than a thousand years later, the Law has become a religious hierarchy rather than a way of life. But Jesus teaches that the Commandments hinge on love. When a teacher of the Law asks Jesus what the most important commandment is, He says, "Love the Lord your God with all your heart and with all your soul and with all your mind and with all your strength. . . . Love your neighbor as yourself" (Mark 12:30–31). Our Father knows that sin will tempt us to live in ways that aren't in line with the identity He calls us to, but love embodied in Jesus is the plumb line that recenters our hearts on who we are in Him.

The Mount of Blessing

With Mount Sinai burned in our minds, I invite you to another mountain. At this mountain, you see a man who is not majestic in appearance. He might blend in with the crowd, but as He looks into your eyes, you feel love and compassion and your soul stirs within you. You sit among the other listeners as He begins to teach about "the way" those that follow Him are to live. (The Early Church identified itself as "The Way.") He opens His mouth and begins to teach you, saying:

> Blessed are the poor in spirit, for theirs is the kingdom of heaven.
> Blessed are those who mourn, for they shall be comforted.
> Blessed are the meek, for they shall inherit the earth.
> Blessed are those who hunger and thirst for righteousness,
> for they shall be satisfied. (Matthew 5:3–6)

Does that refrain sound familiar? "Blessed are those" is used in Psalm 119 and echoed in Jesus' Sermon on the Mount. This language is different from the command from Mount Sinai: "You shall not . . ." One reads like the guidance of a mentor and the other sounds like a statement of fact. So how do we reconcile God on the quaking mountain of Sinai with Jesus, our compassionate Teacher?

The Sacrifice That Leads to Repentance

If you tour the chambers of the House of Representatives in Washington, DC, you will see Moses, who is among twenty-three relief portraits carved into marble and displayed above the gallery doors. This is because some of our lawmakers believed the Ten Commandments God gave Moses have a significant influence on American lawmaking. God's Law is essential in our society and churches, but God wants more than just legal obedience.

When the Israelites break the Law prior to Jesus' sacrifice, God provides a means to transfer their sin and guilt to a sacrifice that will bear their punishment and die in their place. Today, every time we face our inability to keep the letter of the Law, we are driven back to Jesus' sacrifice and forgiveness for us.

Jesus stands on a hill, face-to-face with His followers. He promises blessings for people unsatisfied in this world and hungering for more of God. Then He explains God's greater purpose for the Law, which is accomplished through Him.

Write It on Your Heart

Look up Matthew 5:17. *Do not think that I have come to abolish the Law or the Prophets; I have not come to abolish them but to fulfill them.*

In Jesus, we find an identity that isn't based on our circumstances, abilities, or feelings. This is an identity we can cling to even as our circumstances overwhelm us, our performance falls short, and our emotions threaten to level us. Jesus embodies the Law the Israelites received, living a perfect life in the will of His Father. The most important place we can remember God today is by "looking to Jesus, the founder and perfecter of our faith" (Hebrews 12:2).

INVITATION

How does Jesus offer you rest in the wilderness you are in right now?

DAILY BREAD

Look up Exodus 20:1–21. What qualities do the Ten Commandments reveal about God's character? *just, jealous, loving*

SAY GRACE

Rejoice and be glad, for your reward is great in heaven,
for so they persecuted the prophets who were
before you. (Matthew 5:12)

WEEK 8: DAY 3

The God We Know

Black and red: Egypt is divided into these two colors. *Kremer*, the Egyptian word for "black," is how ancient Egyptians refer to the fertile soil surrounding the Nile. In contrast, the red land is called the *Deshret*, meaning "red crown," which refers to the wilderness desert surrounding Egypt on two sides.[12]

When Moses tells the Israelites that God wants to lead them into the wilderness—the "red land"—he is asking them to do something unheard of! Why would they willingly leave fertile land to go into a land that is wild, barren, and known as a place of danger and death? But after God shows His power over the Egyptian gods through the ten plagues—where He demonstrates His power over water, land, livestock, the sun, and even life and death—they agree to follow Him into the wilderness.

As we studied in Exodus 5, God again outdoes Himself with a water show. In the crescendo of the Israelites' exodus from Egypt, Yahweh parts the sea and then crushes the Egyptian army as the walls of water collapse upon them. Through this wonder, God awesomely delivers and provides for His people and makes a name for Himself in the whole region. Who is this God who allows His people to survive in the wilderness and enables them to thrive and conquer their enemies?

When Moses' father-in-law, Jethro, comes to visit them at Mount Sinai, we learn that he has "heard of all that God had done for Moses and for Israel His people, how the LORD had brought Israel out of Egypt" (Exodus 18:1). Good news travels fast, even in the desert! Jethro responds to this news by proclaiming, "Now I know that the LORD is greater than all gods" (18:11).

A generation later, when Joshua sends spies to scout the Promised Land, the spies end up in Jericho at the house of a prostitute named Rahab. The king of Jericho begins searching for them when he learns they are in the city, but Rahab conceals the men on her roof. Then Rahab offers an alliance with the spies because she has also heard of Israel's awesome God, who brought them stunning victory over their enemies. Rahab says, "For we have heard how the LORD dried up the water of the Red Sea before you when you came out of Egypt." She goes on to recount other Israelite victories in the desert that have been shared in her community, concluding, "As soon as we heard it, our hearts melted, and there was no spirit left in any man because of you, for the LORD your God, He is God in the heavens above and on the earth beneath" (Joshua 2:11).

Yes, among the gods, God is something special. We know, of course, that His power alone makes hearts melt. But what else is it about Yahweh that is so different? There is no comparison between God and the created gods the surrounding nations worshiped, but here are a few things that make Yahweh distinct:

1. The God of Israel reveals His name.

The Hebrew God, Yahweh, comes personally to the Israelites' ancestors Abraham, Isaac, and Jacob. He also comes personally to their leader, Moses, and identifies Himself by name. Their God reveals His character and His name so they can call upon Him for their needs.

The prophet Elijah shows the power of the name of Yahweh when he faces down 450 prophets of Baal, challenging the prophets to prepare sacrifices for their gods to see whose god would send fire: "You call upon the name of your god, and I will call upon the name of the LORD, and the God who answers by fire, He is God" (1 Kings 18:24). The prophets of Baal limp and cry out for hours. They cut themselves with lances and swords so they bleed—to no avail. Then Elijah erects twelve stones for the tribes of Israel, digs a trench, and has it filled with water. Then he prays, "O LORD God of

Abraham, Isaac, and Israel, let it be known this day that You are God in Israel" (18:36). When he finishes his prayer, God's fire consumes the sacrifice and the water. The God we know by name reveals His power to His people.

2. The God of Israel speaks to His people.

When the apostle Paul is in Athens, he is upset to find that the city is full of idols. When the Greek philosophers ask him to tell them about this new teaching he has been presenting in their streets, Paul uses one of their own idols, one that was dedicated "to an unknown god," as the basis for teaching them about Jesus, who came so that God could be made known.

The Greek idol worship is a snapshot of the ancient pursuit across all countries and cultures to not only find god but to gain his favor. "Prayer to Any God," written in ancient Akkadian around the same time as the account of the exodus, originated in ancient Assyria or Babylon. This prayer captures the earnest desire and angst someone feels over their need for the god who will forgive and reconcile them in a relationship.

> May (my) lord's angry heart be reconciled,
>
> May the god I do not know be reconciled,
>
> May the goddess I do not know be reconciled,
>
> May the god, whoever he is, be reconciled,
>
> May the goddess, whoever she is, be reconciled,
>
> O (my) lord, many are my wrongs, great are my sins.[13]

God did not remain unknown but reveals Himself. He hears the cries of His people suffering in Egypt and directs Moses on how they can be freed from slavery and reconciled to Himself. God speaks to us in His Word and Sacraments and through the Holy Spirit, inviting us to know and pray to Him as our Abba, Daddy.

3. The God of Israel blesses His people.

On Mount Sinai, God invites His people into a covenant so He can bless them and help them prosper. Even though all people fail to meet their end of the covenant, God prepares the sacrifice for us in His Son, Jesus, and sends the Holy Spirit fire so we can know Him personally as God and experience His power within us.

A Call to Thrive in Hard Places

God calls us to enter hopeless places or circumstances where we feel helpless. We ask, "Why would You bring us here, God?" His answer isn't always an escape hatch, but somehow He uses these hard places to refine our characters and strengthen our faith. He is more concerned about freeing our hearts from sin than keeping us comfortable in this wilderness. Ultimately, Jesus calls us to thrive in this wilderness world as we walk with Him to our promised land in His eternal presence.

INVITATION

How is God making Himself known to you today?

DAILY BREAD

Look up Romans 5:10–11. How is God different from the gods of other religions? How does this give you hope?

We were reconciled to Him through the death of His Son. How much more, being reconciled, shall we be saved though His life. Reconciliation – Justification through our Lord Jesus Christ.

SAY GRACE

That my glory may sing Your
praise and not be silent. O Lord my God,
I will give thanks to You forever.
(Psalm 30:12)

Idols in Their Hearts

At Mount Sinai, God gives the Israelites the Commandments. Do you remember what that first one says? "You shall have no other gods before Me" (Exodus 20:3). The Israelites can't say they missed that memo. God is very specific regarding what it looks like to have other gods.

Write It on Your Heart

Look up Exodus 20:4. *You shall not make for yourself an idol in the form of anything in heaven above or on the earth beneath or in the waters below.*

Forty days later, the Israelites make a golden calf and worship it. Ugh.

"But why?!" our twenty-first-century hearts cry indignantly. Surely, we would be far more sophisticated than the Israelites and not worship a golden calf. While bovines might not be our brand of worship, like the Israelites, our hearts can also behave as idol-makers. Our idol worship may be more subtle, but it is just as damaging. In my own life, I can read God's Word and remember I am a child of God. And in the next moment, I can obsessively check my Facebook feed for validation and worth. I can worship God and sing "In Christ Alone," but then behave as though my life depends on me alone.

As we strive to keep God at the center of our lives, the lyrics of the hymn "Come, Thou Fount of Every Blessing" resonate with many of us:

Prone to wander, Lord, I feel it;

Prone to leave the God I love.

Here's my heart, O take and seal it,

Seal it for Thy courts above. (*LSB* 686:3)

The definition of an idol is anything that takes priority over God. While that sounds simple on paper (or on a stone tablet), keeping God first in our hearts can be hard to live out as we wrestle with our sinful nature.

We see this with our friends, the Israelites, who struggle with it at Mount Sinai. The other day, we learned about their vow to worship Yahweh alone. So can it be these men and women we read about worshiping and dancing before a cow statue just a month and a half later? Let's look at the story together.

The Israelites have just heard the Ten Commandments from God. Then Moses writes all the words down in the Book of the Covenant, and they sacrifice burnt offerings. He reads the Book of the Covenant to all the people. Together, they say, "All that the LORD has spoken we will do, and we will be obedient" (Exodus 24:7). Moses seals their covenant with the Lord by taking the blood from the sacrifices and putting it on the people. Then Moses, Aaron, and seventy of the elders of Israel go up the mountain. There, "they saw the God of Israel" and have a meal in His presence (24:10–11). The leaders actually see and spend time with God! That makes what comes next even harder to imagine.

After they return to camp, the Lord tells Moses to go up the mountain. He stays there to receive the stone tablets. Before he goes up, Moses leaves Aaron and Hur in charge. How badly can Aaron mess things up while Moses is away? Apparently, very badly. After Moses had been gone for forty days and forty nights, the people go to Aaron and say, "Make us gods who shall go before us. As for this Moses, the man who brought us up out of the land of Egypt, we do not know what has become of him" (32:1). Ouch! And how does Aaron respond? He asks them for the gold rings from their wives, sons, and daughters and makes a golden calf to worship!

Aaron builds an altar where they offer burnt and peace offerings to the calf. Then they eat, drink, and are merry.

As I imagine their sinful revelry, I think indignantly, "How could they?" But that question rings in my ears after I make a choice I promised myself I wouldn't. "How could I?" While the easy answer might be a temptation, desperation, or lack of self-control, I think the more beneficial question we can ask is, "How did I (they) get here?"

Almost nine hundred years later, the problem of idolatry persists. God sends the prophet Ezekiel to tell the Israelites that they "have taken their idols into their hearts, and set the stumbling block of their iniquity before their faces" (Ezekiel 14:3). We can break down Ezekiel's words into two decisions the people of Israel continue to make.

First, they open their hearts to idols.

Sin begins as a thought—either from Satan and the world, or from our own sinful nature. It is a thought we can choose to take captive and hold up against God's truth, or we can agree to partner with the thought. As we agree with our mind, we allow it to grow roots in our hearts, where idolatry truly begins.

The Israelites begin to think God is failing them because Moses hasn't returned from the mountain. They agree with the lie that God isn't faithful and have to take matters into their own hands. Before Aaron forms the golden calf, the people have already committed idolatry when they agree with the lie that they need something to replace God.

Second, they fix their eyes on idols.

In the time of Ezekiel and at Mount Sinai, the people place the idol or idols in the most prominent place. The things we fix our eyes on, the things we touch and see most, might indicate the most important things in our lives. Once their hearts agree to sin, they comply with Aaron. They give him the gold they are wearing so he can make the golden calf, which they put on an altar in a prominent place in the camp so they can look at it often.

We can profess what is most important in our lives, but our hearts lay bare the truth of our devotion. What do we spend our time thinking about? What do we look at with our eyes and put in prominent places in our lives?

Jesus' sacrifice allows us to come to the altar daily as the Holy Spirit helps us change our minds and renew our hearts, remembering that Jesus should be in the center of our lives. We know it's not a pass-fail test. Instead, it is an opportunity to grow in God's free grace for us.

When gold comes out of the earth, it is not the shiny yellow we are familiar with. It is filled with impurities that dull its beauty. As the fire refines the gold, it melts, and the impurities come to the surface. In wilderness seasons, our character is refined as our flaws and insecurities either define us or are refined out of us. In their wilderness at Sinai, the gold God gifted the Israelites in Egypt becomes their hope instead of the living God. May we, in our seasons of waiting and uncertainty, allow Jesus to purify us as we keep our hearts and eyes on Him.

INVITATION

What are the things you spend a lot of time looking at (e.g., your phone, your Bible, your children, the news, etc.).

Books, TV, music

Which of these can become a temptation or distraction? What helps you keep your heart centered on God?

TV - because of the garbage it portrays - Choose Christian shows - books - walk away when it doesn't represent my values

DAILY BREAD

Look up Colossians 3:1–17. Paul says to "set your minds on things above" and "not on things that are on earth." What does this look like in our everyday lives?

Constantly be thinking "What would Jesus do?" So to focus our minds + hearts on God's plans for us.

SAY GRACE

The one who offers thanksgiving
as his sacrifice glorifies Me;
to one who orders his way rightly
I will show the salvation of God!
(Psalm 50:23)

The True Manna

When I polled my community on social media about the wilderness seasons they are going through, they shared heavy things. Life is tiring enough without the struggles that take our breath away and continue to weigh on us for longer than we feel we can carry them. But they pile on anyway. We have struggles such as having a child with ongoing medical issues, losing a spouse or parent, infidelity, job loss, chronic illness, a friend who takes his or her life, and fractures in close relationships. Many of the people who responded to my poll echoed the same wilderness that all of us are in, feeling winded from navigating a "new normal" in our society due to the ongoing uncertainty of the COVID-19 pandemic, heightened political tension, economic woes, and war. As I work through my anxieties and fear about what's happening in the world and what's ahead for my family, I am reminded again that Jesus "Himself is our peace" (Ephesians 2:14). This doesn't mean that He gives us peace, though He does. It means His presence embodies peace. It's not a fleeting, feel-good thought or something I need to strive for. Jesus, God in the flesh, faces the wilderness and conquers it. Into our wilderness, into our doubts and fickle feelings, Jesus has come.

Jesus says, "In the world you will have tribulation" (John 16:33). Synonyms for *tribulation* include *struggle*, *trouble*, *problems*, *anxiety*, *burdens*, and *worry*. Some of you are living with one or more tribulations now. All of us must anticipate loss and struggle. At some point, we are challenged to ask the same question as the Israelites: "Am I going to trust God to provide for me even when the circumstances appear hopeless?" Trust isn't a token we toss into a fountain on a whim. Instead, trust is a response to the faith God has given us as we accept His invitation to follow Him every day. When we pray, "Give us this day our daily bread," we pray for more than shallow comfort or physical needs; we pray for a relationship with Jesus that sustains us in every way.

> And my God will supply every need of yours according to His riches in glory in Christ Jesus. (Philippians 4:19)

Where Are You?

God is faithful and available daily, but as humans, we can get distracted, get discouraged, and doubt God's heart for us. Ultimately, we can choose to live in a relationship with God or muscle through life on our own. In Genesis 1, God created man and woman to live in a relationship and total dependence on Him.

When Eve and Adam chose to try to gain wisdom and ate the apple, it was like smashing a snow globe. What was once whole and perfect became scattered and dangerous. God searched for them, but Adam and Eve felt exposed and hid from God's presence. In their broken condition, God was too holy and perfect to live with them face-to-face. He shed the first blood in creation to cover them in animal skin.

Despite man's sin and separation, God formed a plan to create a people that are set apart for Him. This began with Abraham and grew to a people the size of a nation. But in Exodus, we are introduced to God's people in a predicament. They are slaves in Egypt, unable to remove the burden that Pharaoh has placed on them. God has divinely put Moses in the right place and time to be His messenger, offering the people an exit plan. But the path to escape isn't a set of directions. Instead, it is an invitation to relationship and reliance on God. In the wilderness, God demonstrates to Israel who He is as He fully displays the contrast between man's helplessness and His sufficiency.

While God has a Promised Land prepared for them on the other side of the wilderness, He is showing them more than a physical destination. The wilderness is a place to experience our need for God and encounter

His overwhelming provision and heart for us. Stripped of everyday comfort and distraction, the wilderness tests the devotion of our hearts, but ultimately, the wilderness exposes that we cannot pass through it with our own strength or abilities.

Tabernacle as a Verb

In the final chapters of Exodus, God's plan for reconciliation begins. The Israelites are to construct a dwelling place for God, a tabernacle where He will live again in the center of His people. The instructions God gives Moses for the tabernacle are extensive and include details down to the furnishings and clothing of the priests, as well as the ceremonies, sacrifices, and rituals. Through the tabernacle and system of sacrifice, God is foreshadowing a greater need and the ultimate solution for God to have a relationship with His people.

Ultimately, we need a sacrifice greater than what we can offer. God makes Himself flesh to tabernacle with us in human form. Jesus lives a life that demonstrates how God's sacrificial love and power overcome this wilderness world. God doesn't take us out of the world but invites us to live in it with love and authority

---

JESUS IS THE FINAL SACRIFICE

Old Covenant: Established between God and Israel with Moses as the mediator, the Old Covenant consisted of the Ten Commandments and the laws in Leviticus, which included a system of animal sacrifices. At Mount Sinai, God confirmed the Israelites as His people and promised to grant them prosperity and protection in the Promised Land.

Exodus 24:8. And Moses took the blood and threw it on the people and said:

New Covenant: God accomplished His ultimate solution for sin in Jesus, the perfect Lamb of God, who became the final sacrifice for the forgiveness of our sins and overcame death in His resurrection. Jesus replaced Moses as the mediator between God and us. Instead of prosperity, our great High Priest, Jesus, promises forgiveness of sins and eternal life.

Read Hebrews 8:13.

Read Hebrews 10:11.

---

not of this world. As our bodies cry out in hunger, thirst, and pain, as we walk through this wilderness life of sin and struggle, we look to Jesus, who shows us that the best gift God could give us is Himself.

The Israelites receive a foretaste of heaven's provision in manna. Today, we receive Jesus, the bread of life, broken so we could be made whole.

INVITATION

What are three key takeaways that you want to remember from this study?

1.

2.

3.

DAILY BREAD

Look up Exodus 40:34–37 and John 1:14. What strikes you about how these verses are similar? How are these verses different? What does this demonstrate about God? God is with us.

SAY GRACE

And I heard every creature in heaven and on earth and under the earth and in the sea, and all that is in them, saying, "To Him who sits on the throne and to the Lamb be blessing and honor and glory and might forever and ever!" (Revelation 5:13)

EPILOGUE

The Ultimate Promised Land

As I work on the final details of this book, I'm getting distracted by mixed emotions. My friend recently shared that her workplace was in lockdown due to an active shooter in Tulsa, Oklahoma, where four people were killed. A week before that, a man went into an elementary school in Uvalde, Texas, and killed nineteen children and two teachers. Ten people were killed in a supermarket in Buffalo, New York, two weeks prior to the shooting in Texas.

The brokenness of this world feels sharper and more painful than usual as I try to process the hate and brutality that destroys the innocent with no regard. On social media platforms and in the news, people are processing their grief with an outcry for gun control, more access to mental health resources, and more security. These conversations are important, but they feel like a Band-Aid to cover the gaping wound of evil that would motivate someone to commit these heinous acts in the first place. As Christians, we know the true source of evil:

> Be sober-minded; be watchful. Your adversary the devil prowls
> around like a roaring lion, seeking someone to devour. (1 Peter 5:8)

The world feels like a dangerous place. When evil crashes into our schools and supermarkets, that's more apparent than ever. The enemy prowls around, wanting to devour our innocence, trust, confidence, and hearts. As we face this world's injustice, however, we do not need to engage in the world's arena. Our cunning arguments and moralism will not defeat this enemy. Instead, we pray, "Your kingdom come, Your will be done, on earth as it is in heaven," clinging to the promise that Jesus has overcome this wilderness world (Matthew 6:10). As we endure pain, loss, depression, and any struggle that threatens to separate us from God, we look to Jesus, who has ultimately defeated sin, death, and the devil and prepares a place for us in the promised land of heaven with Him. God's eternity is planted within our hearts as we live in this broken world. His future reality comes crashing into our lives daily as we partner with Him to usher in God's restoration, forgiveness, and healing.

The ultimate promised land cannot be attained through our solutions, our striving, best behavior, or a human blueprint. It is only through our Baptism, as we confess Jesus as our Savior, that we take this unconventional path to a future He prepares for us. God's ultimate promise isn't to float to heaven on a cloud either. God's ultimate vision for His people is to dwell with us in a real-world, with seeds and soil, heavenly bodies of flesh and blood, God's creation, pure and new, no longer muted and darkened by the curse nor tainted by evil. God's ultimate promise is for all nations to acknowledge Jesus as God's own Son and Savior so that we, like our ancestors, might "desire a better country, that is, a heavenly one" (Hebrews 11:16). As we remember that we are still seeking a homeland, we wait in this wilderness world with anticipation for the city God has prepared for us where He will "shelter [us] with His presence" (Revelation 7:15).

> Then I saw a new heaven and a new earth, for the first heaven and the first earth had passed away, and the sea was no more. And I saw the holy city, new Jerusalem, coming down out of heaven from God, prepared as a bride adorned for her husband. And I heard a loud voice from the throne saying, "Behold, the dwelling place of God is with man. He will dwell with them, and they will be His people, and God Himself will be with them as their God. He will wipe every tear from their eyes, and death shall be no more, neither shall there be mourning, nor crying, nor pain anymore, for the former things have passed away." (Revelation 21:1–4)

In Gratitude

I failed to include acknowledgments in my first book, so I am catching up here!

A special thank you to the team at CPH for making my ideas into something special, especially Peggy Kuethe. Working with you is so encouraging and such a joy. You make my words sparkle. Elizabeth Pittman, thank you for your expertise, guidance, and support.

To Molly Dixon and the ladies at Grace Space, your love for the Lord and commitment to studying God's Word inspires me.

Fellow authors Michelle Diercks, Deb Burma, and the other lovely CPH authors, your generous support is so encouraging. I look forward to working together more and seeing all the ways God will continue to shine through you!

To my friends at Thrive Book Club (Rachel, Carolyn, Marianne, Kelly, Nicole, Emma, Mary Louise, Renee, Sheri, Kim, Kathryn, and the list goes on), you all are such an inspiration to me. I think of you as I'm writing every book.

My friends at PLI, thank you for leading well and inspiring us to lead from within.

Ursula Sohns, you are my number one cheerleader!

Laurie Kluenker and Sheri Woods, you are wonderful friends who point me to Jesus every day.

I also want to thank my beautiful kids and patient and supportive husband.

To my family, especially Danielle and Patria, thank you for showing me how to navigate the wilderness with grace and perseverance. Thanks also to Erin for being my big sis who has helped me through quite a few wildernesses.

I'm also grateful for my Hausch family members, who are dotted across the country. I'm honored to carry on the family name.

References

Appel, Timothy. "Sharper Iron & The Saga of Salvation: Christ, Our Passover Lamb." KFUO. Accessed June 8, 2022. https://www.kfuo.org/2019/08/05/sharperiron-saga-salvation-080519-christ-our-passover-lamb/.

Architect of the Capital. "Relief Portrait Plaques of Lawgivers." Accessed April 1, 2022. https://www.aoc.gov/explore-capitol-campus/art/relief-portrait-plaques-lawgivers.

Blue Letter Bible. "Dictionary and Word Search for yir'ah (Strong's 3374)." Accessed March 24, 2022. https://www.blueletterbible.org/lexicon/h3374/esv/wlc/0-1/.

Concordia Publishing House blog. "Exodus and God's Law." Accessed March 8, 2022. https://blog.cph.org/study/exodus-and-gods-law.

Deffinbaugh, Bob. "12. Saul and the Amalekites (1 Samuel 15:1–35)." Accessed May 13, 2022. https://bible.org/seriespage/12-saul-and-amalekites-1-samuel-151-35.

DeJong, George. "With God in Wild Places Ep. 1: Mikdash." Under the Fig Tree Ministries. September 18, 2019. Video, 15:22. https://www.youtube.com/watch?v=clzeJ_7-Qy8.

Godet, Frédéric Louis. "Godet's Commentary on Selected Books: 1 Corinthians 10." Accessed January 18, 2022. https://www.studylight.org/commentaries/eng/gsc/1-corinthians-10.html.

Hubbard, Scott. "God Awakens Us in the Wilderness." Desiring God. Accessed June 9, 2022. https://www.desiringgod.org/articles/god-awakens-us-in-the-wilderness.

Imes, Carmen Joy. *Bearing God's Name: Why Sinai Still Matters*. Downers Grove, IL: Intervarsity Press, 2019.

Lindsey, Gordon. "The Exodus as a Creation Story." Accessed January 18, 2022. https://thebibleisinmyblood.wordpress.com/2018/09/27/the-exodus-as-a-creation-story/.

Silberman, Ran. "'The Word' (Λόγος) and the 'Wilderness.'" Accessed January 5, 2022. https://ransilberman.blog/2020/07/18/the-word-λόγος-and-the-wilderness/.

Solomon, Marty. "Images of the Desert—Shepherd." Produced by BEMA Discipleship. The BEMA Podcast, April 6, 2017. Podcast, 36:22. https://www.bemadiscipleship.com/26.

Endnotes

1   "Biblical Vocabulary: The Word דּוֹבָּכ (God's Honor and Glory), Part 1," Biblword (website), accessed February 23, 2022, https://www .biblword.net/biblical-vocabulary-gods-honor-and-glory-part-1/.

2   Martin Luther, *What Luther Says* (St. Louis: Concordia Publishing House, 1959), § 3457.

3   Oswald Chambers, "The Philosophy of Sin," in *The Complete Works of Oswald Chambers.* (Grand Rapids, MI: Oswald Chambers Publications Assn., Ltd., 2000), 111.

4   Poem by Lindsay Hausch.

5   Martin Luther, *Luther's Works*, vol. 27, *Lectures on Galatians* (Concordia Publishing House, St. Louis, 2007), 289.

6   "Thirsty Souls," original poem by the author. © 2022 Lindsay Hausch.

7   Chambers, *My Utmost for His Highest* (Grand Rapids, MI: Oswald Chambers Publications Assn., Ltd., 1963), March 19.

8   *Merriam-Webster.com Dictionary*, s.v. "provide," accessed November 4, 2022, https://www.merriam-webster.com/dictionary/provide.

9   *Merriam-Webster.com Dictionary*, s.v. "sustain," accessed November 4, 2022, https://www.merriam-webster.com/dictionary/sustain.

10   "Reflection on Isaiah 60 and Psalm 81:10," poem by Lindsay Hausch. © 2022 Lindsay Hausch.

11   *Random House Webster's College Dictionary*, 2nd ed. (New York: Random House, 1998), s.v. "covenant."

12   "Deshret," Academic (website), accessed March 18, 2022, https:// en-academic.com/dic.nsf/enwiki/1073051.

13   Benjamin R. Foster, "Prayer to Any God," in *Before the Muses* (CDL Press, 1996), 670.

14   "Reflection on Isaiah 60 and Psalm 81:10," poem by Lindsay Hausch. © 2022 Lindsay Hausch.